THOMAS LAIRD

false hustle

Transforming Customer Experience from Illusion to Impact

eXpivia

Contents

Prologue

You're about to dive into a book that hopefully challenges everything you thought you knew about serving customers in your contact center. The insights, strategies, and hard-earned lessons within these pages stem from decades of experience at the forefront of the contact center industry, where every call and every interaction shapes the customer experience.

Let me be clear right from the start: If you're the type who believes in cutting contact center costs at any expense, getting rid of agents, and strictly adhering to efficiency metrics above all else, this book isn't for you. Close it now, send me a direct message on LinkedIn, and I'll personally refund your purchase. But, if you're a contact center or CX manager or executive who is frustrated that your team isn't delivering the service your customers deserve, and you're looking for real answers and solutions, then you're in the right place.

This approach is much more challenging to implement than current practices, which is why few companies attempt it and service quality often suffers. I acknowledge that it may not be suitable for every organization. However, if you fully embrace this method, it will fundamentally change how customers perceive your company and how the right employees view their roles.

Didn't scare you off yet :) OK lets go!

This is my fourth book, and with each one, my goal has been to challenge conventional wisdom and push the boundaries of what's possible in the customer experience space.

For those who know me or have followed my content, the concept of "false hustle" (which we'll dive into in the following chapters) is something I've been passionate about for years. Whether through my writing, public speaking, or on my podcast, "Advice from a Call Center Geek," I've been on a mission to expose the misguided practices that plague our industry and promote a more authentic, effective approach to customer service.

As the CEO of Expivia, a 600-seat USA contact center outsourcer, I've seen firsthand how the relentless drive for efficiency can overshadow our true purpose: delivering genuine value to customers.

Recognizing the untapped potential in automated quality assurance, I also founded OttoQA, a company that leverages AI to transform how contact centers handle QA. But OttoQA is about more than just scoring quality forms, it's about using technology to enhance the human touch, ensuring that every customer interaction is meaningful and impactful.

Now, let's talk about AI. Yes, I used AI in writing this book. And darn right I did! Think of it as my free editor, the tool that helped fix my grammar and make my voice clearer. AI allowed me to organize and refine my thoughts more efficiently, but make no mistake, the ideas, strategies, and experiences shared here are all mine, cultivated over years in the contact center world. The AI was just a tool; the heart and soul of this book remain rooted in my real-world experiences. If you follow my content, you know this.

While technology has been improving every year, customer service has been on a steady decline. From 2017 through the pandemic, customer satisfaction has dropped despite these advances. It's clear that technology alone isn't the full answer. While it can enhance efficiency and support agents, it doesn't replace the need for genuine, human-centered service.

This is where combating false hustle becomes crucial. It's not just about using the latest tools; it's about ensuring those tools foster real connections and solve actual problems, rather than just creating the appearance of productivity.

This book is the culmination of everything I've learned and shared over the years, now brought together in a comprehensive exploration of how false hustle undermines genuine customer service and, more importantly, how we can overcome it.

You'll find themes and concepts I've discussed in podcast episodes, previous books, and speaking engagements, but taken further, providing a deeper dive into the problem of false hustle and offering concrete solutions for transforming contact centers into hubs of authentic customer experience.

As you read, you'll see that the essence of this book is pure, unfiltered "call center geek." It's the distillation of years spent thinking about, experimenting with, and championing better ways to serve customers and empower contact center employees. Whether through the innovative practices at Expivia, the cutting-edge technology of OttoQA, or the insights shared on my podcast, my goal has always been the same: to elevate the role of contact centers from mere cost centers to strategic assets that drive real business growth.

Let's embark on this journey together, moving beyond false hustle to create contact centers that truly put customers first. Welcome to the revolution in customer service, its all here...

Tom Laird

CEO Expivia/OttoQa

8/28/2024

Introduction

Introduction: Breaking the False Hustle Cycle in Contact Centers and CX

In the high-stakes arena of modern business, where customer loyalty can make or break a company, contact centers stand as the frontline warriors in the battle for customer satisfaction. Yet, despite their critical role, many contact centers unknowingly sabotage their own efforts through a pervasive phenomenon I've come to call "false hustle." This book is your roadmap to identifying, understanding, and eliminating false hustle, paving the way for a revolution in how we approach customer experience (CX) and contact center operations.

As we stand on the brink of an AI revolution in customer service, it's more crucial than ever to understand the value of authentic, *unscripted human interactions*. It will be a monster advantage for certain companies that understand this.

The companies that will thrive in this new landscape are those that can seamlessly blend AI efficiency with the irreplaceable human touch. They're the ones who recognize that while AI can handle routine inquiries with lightning speed, it's the human agents who can navigate complex issues, show genuine empathy, and create the kind of memorable experiences that build lasting customer loyalty.

As the next couple years go by, every company will have AI handling a portion of their customer service, but not everyone will have the kind of agents who can excel when AI takes over the routine questions and leaves the complex ones, with the ticked off customer that AI can't handle.

AI won't be the differentiator; companies that understand how to cultivate genuine human conversation and connection will be. It's a familiar story, isn't it? Just like the last 50 years, the human element remains key to true customer experience success.

Throughout my career, I've witnessed the evolution of customer service from simple phone interactions to complex, omni-channel experiences. I've seen strategies come and go, technologies rise and fall, but one constant remains: the fundamental importance of genuine human connection in delivering exceptional customer experiences.

My journey in the world of contact centers began on the front lines as an agent, where I first encountered the seeds of what I now recognize as false hustle. As I climbed the ranks to management and eventually to my role as a founder and CEO, I've had a unique vantage point to observe how this insidious practice takes root and spreads throughout contact centers and management, often with the best of intentions but the worst of outcomes.

"false hustle" Defined

But what exactly is **"false hustle"** in the context of customer service?

At its core, false hustle is the misguided effort to appear productive and efficient at the expense of actually solving customer problems and building meaningful relationships.

It's the robotic adherence to scripts that ignore the nuances of individual customer needs. It's the over obsession with efficiency metrics like average handle time that overlook the quality of the interaction. It's the pressure to close tickets quickly rather than resolve issues thoroughly. Its fake scripted empathy, its saying thank you ten times on a call, its telling agents to say the customers name four times in the fist two minutes of the call and calling that 'engagement'.

False hustle manifests in many ways: agents rushing through calls to meet quotas, managers focusing on superficial performance metrics rather than customer outcomes, and organizations implementing policies that prioritize speed over satisfaction. The result? Frustrated customers, burned-out employees, and a *disconnect between the service a company thinks it's providing and the experience customers actually receive.* (You know you have this in your center and you have thought about it.)

The objective of this book is nothing short of revolutionary: to transform how contact centers operate and how businesses approach customer experience. Pretty bold huh!!

We'll embark on a journey to dismantle the false hustle mindset and rebuild contact centers as engines of genuine customer satisfaction and business growth.

This book is structured to guide you through a comprehensive transformation of your contact center operations:

First we'll dive deep into understanding false hustle and its impact. We'll explore its manifestations, the disconnect it creates between brands and customers, and the crucial importance of effective customer management.

You'll learn to identify false hustle in your own operations and understand its costly consequences.

Next we will focus on strategies for a customer-centric approach. We'll cover proven techniques for calming irate customers, methods for active listening and tailoring experiences, and strategies for adapting CX approaches across different industries.

This section will equip you with practical tools to create authentic, empathetic customer interactions.

After learning that, we'll tackle the challenge of building a truly customer-centric organization. We'll explore how to hire and onboard emotionally intelligent agents, implement comprehensive quality assurance processes for service, retention, and sales calls, and optimize your operations for customer satisfaction. This section provides a blueprint for transforming your contact center from the ground up.

Finally we will, introduces advanced QA techniques and technology. We'll explore the evolution of call center QA, including the game-changing potential of Automated Quality Assurance (Auto QA). You'll learn how to leverage the Law of Large Numbers in your QA process, enabling you to maintain high standards of quality even as you scale your operations.

Throughout these pages, we'll draw on real-world examples, data-driven insights, and proven strategies that we have developed and refined over my decades in the industry. We'll explore the psychology of customer service, examining what drives both customer and employee behavior. We'll also look at cutting-edge technologies and methodologies that can support, rather than supplant, the human element of customer interaction.

This book is designed for a wide audience: contact center managers looking to optimize their operations, executives seeking to transform their customer experience strategy, frontline agents aiming to enhance their skills, and even customers curious about what goes on behind the scenes of their service interactions. Whether you're a seasoned professional or new to the field, you'll find insights and strategies you can implement immediately to improve your approach to customer service.

By the time you finish this book, you'll have a comprehensive toolkit for transforming your contact center into a powerhouse of customer satisfaction and loyalty. You'll understand how to create an environment where both customers and employees thrive, driving not just customer retention but also business growth. You'll be equipped to leverage cutting-edge technologies like Auto QA while maintaining the human touch that's essential to truly outstanding customer service.

The path to revolutionizing contact centers and CX is not an easy one. It requires a fundamental shift in mindset, a willingness to challenge established norms, and a commitment to putting the customer at the center of every decision. But for those who embark on this journey, the rewards are immense: happier customers, more engaged employees, and a stronger, more resilient business.

So, let's begin this transformative journey together. It's time to break the cycle of false hustle and usher in a new era of authentic, effective, and truly satisfying customer service. Welcome to the future of contact center operations and customer experience.

1

False Hustle: From the Basketball Court to the Contact Center

You know, sometimes the biggest business insights come from the most unexpected places. For me, the concept of "false hustle" didn't originate in a boardroom or a management seminar. It hit me like a slam dunk while I was coaching basketball.

Picture this: I'm on the sidelines, watching my team during a game. There's this one kid on the court, arms flailing, feet stomping, looking like he's giving 110%. But here's the thing - he's not actually accomplishing anything. He's not in the right position, not making the right plays, just... hustling for the sake of hustling.

That's when it hit me. This kid was the perfect embodiment of what I'd been seeing in contact centers for years. Agents who looked busy, sounded busy, but weren't actually solving customer problems. Managers pushing for higher numbers without considering the quality of interactions. Executives implementing policies that created a lot of activity but little actual progress.

I called it "false hustle" on the basketball court, and I realized it was exactly what was plaguing the customer service industry.

The Basketball Connection: True Hustle vs. False Hustle

Let's dive deeper into this basketball analogy because it really illuminates the essence of false hustle in customer service.

In basketball, true hustle means being in the right place at the right time. It means making smart plays, supporting your teammates, and always keeping the end goal in mind - winning the game. It's not about who runs the most or jumps the highest; it's about who contributes most effectively to the team's success.

I remember coaching a game where we were up against a team that, on paper, should have wiped the floor with us. But we had a secret weapon: a point guard who understood true hustle. She wasn't the fastest or the strongest, but she had an uncanny ability to anticipate where the ball was going to be. She set up her teammates for success, made smart passes, and played stellar defense. We won that game not because we out-hustled the other team, but because we hustled smart.

Now, contrast that with false hustle on the court. It's the player who's always running, always shouting, always looking busy - but rarely in the right position. It's the player who dives for a ball that's already out of bounds, or the one who takes wild shots instead of passing to an open teammate. It looks impressive, but it doesn't help the team win.

The same principles apply in customer service. True hustle in a contact center means actively listening to customers, providing thoughtful solutions, and always keeping the end goal in mind - customer satisfaction and loyalty. False hustle, on the other hand, is all about looking busy without actually solving problems or building relationships.

What is False Hustle in Customer Service?

Just like that well-meaning but misguided basketball player, false hustle in contact centers is all about motion without progress. It's the corporate equivalent of a hamster wheel - lots of energy expended, but no real distance covered.

In the world of customer service, false hustle manifests in countless ways:

- The agent who rushes through calls, more concerned with their average handle time than actually solving the customer's problem.
- The manager who pushes for higher call volumes, ignoring the quality of those interactions.
- The executive who implements strict scripting policies, strangling the natural flow of conversation between agents and customers.
- The QA team that obsesses over checkbox metrics while missing the big picture of customer satisfaction.

- The IT department that implements new technology without considering how it impacts the customer experience.
- The training team that focuses on process adherence rather than developing critical thinking and problem-solving skills.

Let me give you a real-world example. I once consulted for a large telecommunications company that prided itself on its "efficient" customer service. Their average handle time was impressively low, and their agents were handling a high volume of calls each day. On paper, it looked great. But when we dug deeper, we found that their customer satisfaction scores were in the toilet, and their repeat call rate was through the roof.

Why? Because their agents were so focused on keeping calls short that they weren't actually resolving customer issues. They were ending calls quickly, sure, but customers were hanging up frustrated and having to call back again and again. That's false hustle in action, folks.

The Psychology Behind False Hustle

Now, you might be wondering, why do smart, well-intentioned people fall into the trap of false hustle? The answer lies in the psychology of human behavior and the way we structure our organizations.

The Illusion of Productivity

There's a cognitive bias called the "labor illusion," where people tend to value effort over results. In customer service, this translates to valuing busy-ness over effectiveness. It feels good to tick off tasks quickly, even if those tasks don't actually solve the customer's problem.

Metric Fixation

In many contact centers, we've become obsessed with more measurable efficiency metrics. Things like average handle time, ASA, and scoring adherence to script are easy to measure, so we focus on them. But as the saying goes, "Not everything that counts can be counted, and not everything that can be counted counts."

Short-Term Thinking

False hustle often provides short-term gains. You can handle more calls in a day, which looks great on the daily report. But it ignores the long-term costs of customer dissatisfaction and churn.

Fear and Insecurity

In high-pressure environments, employees might engage in false hustle out of fear. They want to look busy and productive to keep their jobs, even if their actions aren't truly beneficial.

Misaligned Incentives

If we reward employees for the wrong things (like sheer volume of calls handled or high QA scores on a flawed scorecard), we shouldn't be surprised when they optimize for those metrics at the expense of actual customer service.

Understanding these psychological factors is crucial because it helps us see that false hustle isn't usually the result of laziness or malice. It's often well-intentioned people trying their best in a system that's inadvertently set up to reward the wrong behaviors.

The Origins of False Hustle in Contact Centers

To truly understand false hustle, we need to look at its origins in the contact center industry. This isn't a new problem - it's been baked into the way we operate for decades.

In the early days of contact centers, efficiency reigned supreme. The focus was on getting customers off the phone as quickly as possible, giving birth to metrics like average handle time (AHT), calls per hour, and talk time. While these metrics have their place, we lost sight of their true purpose. Instead of viewing them as indicators of a larger picture, they became the end goal themselves.

Reflecting on my early days in the industry during the late '80s, I recall a time of rotary phones and paper logs. Even then, the seeds of false hustle were being sown. As efficiency metrics took hold, the human element began to erode. Agents were pushed

16

to handle more calls faster, often at the expense of actually helping customers.

The outsourcing boom further exacerbated the problem. Contact centers managed by people who had never set foot in the parent company's offices prioritized raw efficiency over customer understanding. The misguided belief was that paying bottom dollar for agents necessitated squeezing every second of productivity from them.

This relentless drive for efficiency and metric obsession has led us astray. We've lost sight of what truly matters: human connection. Despite technological advancements, customer satisfaction has steadily declined since 2017, even through the pandemic. It's clear that technology alone isn't the full answer.

The Cost of False Hustle

Now, you might be thinking, "Tom, what's the big deal? So what if we're a little too focused on efficiency? Isn't that good for the bottom line?"

Here's the reality: false hustle is costing your business more than you can imagine. Let's break it down:

Customer Churn

When customers feel like they're talking to a wall instead of a human, they walk. And in today's world, they don't just walk - they run straight to your competitors, all while telling everyone on social media about their horrible experience. I've seen companies lose millions in revenue due to customer churn caused by poor service.

Employee Burnout

Your agents are on the front lines, day in and day out. When you force them into this false hustle mindset, you're essentially asking them to check their humanity at the door. The result? High turnover, low morale, and a team that's just going through the motions. And let me tell you, the cost of constantly recruiting and training new agents is staggering.

Missed Opportunities

Every customer interaction is a goldmine of information - if you're willing to listen. But when you're hustling your agents off the phone as quickly as possible, you're missing out on valuable insights that could drive product improvements, identify new market opportunities, or nip emerging issues in the bud. I once worked with a company that discovered a major product flaw only after they slowed down and started really listening to their customers. That discovery saved them millions in potential lawsuits.

Brand Damage

In the age of viral tweets and online reviews, a single bad customer experience can spiral into a PR nightmare. False hustle creates these bad experiences in spades. I've seen brands that took decades to build get seriously damaged in a matter of days due to poor customer service practices.

Ineffective Problem Solving

When you're more concerned with closing tickets than actually solving problems, guess what happens? Those problems come back, again and again, like a bad penny. You're not saving time - you're just kicking the can down the road. This leads to increased call volumes, frustrated customers, and a never-ending cycle of inefficiency.

Compliance Risks

In many industries, especially highly regulated ones like finance and healthcare, rushing through customer interactions can lead to serious compliance issues. I've seen companies face hefty fines and legal troubles because their false hustle approach led to mistakes in handling sensitive customer information.

The Technology Trap

Now, I want to touch on something that I see a lot of companies falling into - what I call the "technology trap." In an effort to improve efficiency and reduce costs, many organizations are turning to AI, chatbots, and other technological solutions. And don't get me wrong, these tools can be incredibly powerful when used correctly.

But here's the thing: too often, these technologies become just another form of false hustle. Companies implement them as a quick fix, a way to handle more customer interactions with fewer human agents. But they forget the most important part of the equation - the customer experience.

I once worked with a company that was proud of their new AI-powered chatbot. It could handle a huge volume of customer inquiries, and it had slashed their call volume. But when we looked at their customer satisfaction scores, they had tanked. Why? Because the chatbot was great at handling simple, straightforward requests, but it was terrible at understanding context, nuance, or complex issues. Customers were getting frustrated, feeling like they were talking to a brick wall.

The kicker? When we calculated the lifetime value of the customers they were losing, it dwarfed the money they were saving on call center costs. Their "efficiency" was costing them millions in lost revenue and brand damage.

Breaking the Cycle

Just like in basketball, breaking bad habits in customer service isn't easy. It requires a fundamental shift in how we think about performance, success, and the very purpose of customer interactions.

In the coming chapters, we're going to explore strategies for dismantling the false hustle mentality and building a contact center that truly serves your customers, your employees, and your bottom line.

We'll explore how to:

- Redefine your metrics to focus on what really matters

- Train your agents to have genuine, human conversations
- Leverage technology to enhance, not replace, the human touch
- Build a culture of empathy and problem-solving
- Implement quality assurance processes that drive real improvement
- Create a feedback loop that turns customer insights into actionable improvements
- Develop leadership strategies that prioritize true customer service over false efficiency

But before we get there, I want you to do something for me. Take a hard look at your contact center. Are you seeing signs of false hustle? Are your agents rushing through calls? Are your managers more concerned with numbers than outcomes? Are your customers leaving interactions feeling frustrated and unheard?

If you answered yes to any of these questions, don't worry. You're not alone. The good news is, you've taken the first step by recognizing the problem. And trust me, by the time you finish this book, you'll have all the tools you need to transform your contact center from a hub of false hustle to a powerhouse of genuine customer satisfaction.

In the next chapter, we'll dig deeper into the specific manifestations of false hustle in contact centers, and start to explore strategies for identifying and addressing these issues in your own organization. We'll look at real-world case studies, both successes and failures, to illustrate the impact of false hustle and the power of true customer-centric service.

So, are you ready to change the game? Let's do this. It's time to trade in that false hustle for the real deal, and start delivering the kind of customer service that builds loyalty, drives growth, and makes your organization stand out in a crowded marketplace.

2

Spotting the Smoke and Mirrors: How to Identify False Hustle in Your Contact Center

False hustle is the appearance of productivity without actual effectiveness. It's when your agents are busy, your metrics look good on paper, QA score are high, but your customers are left unsatisfied and your employees are burning out. It's a chameleon, adapting to different environments and hiding in plain sight. But once you know what to look for, you'll start seeing it everywhere.

In this chapter, we're going to put on our detective hats and learn how to spot false hustle in action. We'll explore its common manifestations, understand how our traditional practices might be inadvertently encouraging it, and examine the steep costs of ignoring this problem. By the end of this chapter, you'll be equipped with the knowledge to identify false hustle in your own contact center – the first crucial step in eradicating it.

The Vicious Nature of False Hustle

False hustle is particularly dangerous because it often masquerades as dedication and efficiency. It can be difficult to recognize, especially when your traditional metrics are telling you that everything is fine. But make no mistake, false hustle is a silent killer of customer satisfaction and employee morale.

Let's explore why false hustle is so persistent in contact centers:

1. **Short-term Focus**: Many contact centers are under pressure to deliver immediate results. This can lead to an emphasis on quick fixes and surface-level solutions that look good in the short term but create long-term problems.
2. **Misaligned Incentives**: When we reward behaviors that promote false hustle (like extremely low handle times or high call volumes), we're inadvertently encouraging agents to prioritize speed over quality.
3. **Fear of Change**: Some organizations resist changing their processes or metrics out of fear that it might disrupt their operations or negatively impact their numbers.
4. **Lack of Customer-Centric Culture**: In centers where the customer's voice isn't prioritized, it's easy for false hustle to thrive unchecked.
5. **Technology Misuse**: While technology can be a powerful tool, it can also enable false hustle when implemented without careful consideration of its impact on the customer experience.

Understanding these factors can help you recognize why false hustle might be present in your organization and guide your efforts to combat it.

Common Manifestations of False Hustle

Now that we understand the origins of false hustle, let's learn how to spot it in action. After decades in this business, I've seen false hustle take many forms. Here are the ten most common manifestations you need to watch out for:

1. **The Speed Demon**: This is the agent who's always bragging about how many calls they can handle in an hour. They're quick, alright, but at what cost? Speed Demons often leave a trail of unresolved issues and confused customers in their wake. They might hit their AHT targets, but their First Call Resolution (FCR) rates are abysmal.

2. **The Script Robot**: You know the type – they stick to the script like it's the holy grail, even when it's clearly not helping the customer. They might hit all the right keywords for the QA team, but they're about as personable as a vending machine. Customers feel like they're talking to a wall, not a person.

3. **The Metric Chaser**: This could be an agent or a manager, always obsessing over the numbers. They're so focused on improving their AHT or FCR that they forget there's a real person on the other end of the line. They might look great on a spreadsheet, but customer satisfaction scores tell a different story.

4. **The Pass-the-Buck Pro**: This agent's favorite phrase is "Let me transfer you." They're experts at getting customers off their line, but not so great at actually solving problems. Sure, their handle times look great, but the

customer is left feeling like a hot potato, passed from one agent to another.

5. **The Surface Skimmer**: They address the surface-level issue but never dig deeper to find the root cause. Sure, they might solve the immediate problem, but the customer will likely be calling back soon with the same issue. It's a band-aid solution that looks good in the short term but creates more problems down the line.

6. **The Checkbox Champion**: They tick all the boxes on the QA scorecard but miss the forest for the trees. They might get a perfect score, but the customer leaves the interaction feeling unheard and unsatisfied. It's a classic case of meeting the letter of the law while completely missing its spirit.

7. **The Runaway Conductor**: This is the agent who consistently lets the customer drive the conversation off the rails. They might think they're being accommodating, but in reality, they're letting calls drag on without resolution, frustrating customers and bloating handle times. It's a case of misplaced empathy that ultimately helps no one.

8. **The Empathy Actor**: They've memorized all the right phrases to sound caring, but there's no genuine feeling behind it. Customers can smell this fake empathy a mile away, and it often leaves them feeling more annoyed than if the agent hadn't tried at all. It's the uncanny valley of customer service – close to genuine empathy, but not quite there, and all the more unsettling for it.

9. **The Data Dodger**: This agent is all about getting through the call as quickly as possible, often at the expense of proper data entry. They might have great handle times, but they're leaving a mess for their colleagues and creating

a nightmare for any future customer interactions. It's a classic case of "not my problem" thinking that creates ripple effects throughout the organization.

10. **The Deflection Master**: Instead of addressing the customer's actual concerns, this agent is an expert at redirecting the conversation to easier topics or solutions that don't quite fit the bill. They might avoid escalations in the short term, but they're breeding long-term customer dissatisfaction. It's conflict avoidance masquerading as problem-solving.

Let me give you a real-world example of false hustle in action.

I once worked with a telecom company where false hustle was running rampant. They had agents who could fly through calls at lightning speed, and their efficiency metrics looked great on paper. The average handle time was low, calls per hour were high, and management was thrilled.

But when we actually listened to the calls, it was a disaster. Customers were getting rushed off the phone before their problems were solved. Agents were robotically reciting scripts without actually listening to the customers' issues. The repeat call rate was through the roof, and customer satisfaction scores were plummeting.

One particularly memorable call involved a customer with a complex billing issue. The agent, clearly a Speed Demon, rushed through the standard troubleshooting script in record time. They ticked all the boxes on the QA scorecard, used all the right

27

empathy statements, and closed the call in under five minutes. On paper, it looked like a perfect call.

But the customer called back the very next day with the same issue. When we dug deeper, we found that while the agent had addressed the surface-level problem, they had completely missed the underlying issue that was causing the recurring billing errors. The customer had to call three more times before the problem was finally resolved.

This is false hustle in action, folks. It looks good on paper, but it's actually creating more problems than it solves.

Traditional QA Scorecards as a Contributor

Now, here's a hard truth that might ruffle some feathers: a lot of the false hustle we see in contact centers is actually encouraged by our traditional QA scorecards. I know, I know, QA is supposed to ensure quality, right? But the road to poor customer service is often paved with good intentions.

Before we dive into the specific issues with traditional scorecards, let's acknowledge a fundamental problem: the human factor in QA scoring. There are inherent limitations we face as humans when it comes to performing repetitive tasks, such as scoring contact center QA calls over and over again. To simplify this process for managers, we often design systems that prioritize efficiency, enabling them to get through as many calls as possible.

Unfortunately, this often results in "scoring to the test," where the focus is on checking boxes rather than deeply analyzing the quality of the interactions. I believe this approach is one of the fundamental reasons why customer experience in many organizations is mediocre at best.

This is also an area where I truly believe AI can have the biggest impact. AI systems can process vast amounts of data without fatigue, potentially offering more consistent and comprehensive evaluations. But that's a topic for a later chapter. For now, let's focus on how our current QA practices contribute to false hustle.

Let's break down how traditional QA scorecards can actually negatively promote false hustle:

Scripting Adherence: Many scorecards have a section for following the script. While scripts can be useful guides, when we score agents on strict adherence, we're discouraging them from having real, human conversations. We're breeding Script Robots who can't adapt to unique customer situations.

Superficial Courtesy Checks: You know those scorecards that give points for saying "please" and "thank you" a certain number of times? They're teaching agents to parrot polite phrases instead of showing genuine care. Hello, Empathy Actors.

Scripted Empathy: Some scorecards require agents to use specific empathy statements, like "I understand how frustrating that must be." While empathy is crucial, forcing agents to use pre-written phrases often results in insincere-sounding interactions that customers can easily detect.

Artificial Engagement Metrics: Scorecards that require agents to use the customer's name a specific number of times (like four times per call) create unnatural conversations. True engagement comes from genuine interaction, not from hitting an arbitrary name-usage quota.

Lack of Problem Resolution Scoring: Many scorecards focus on process adherence but fail to adequately measure whether the customer's issue was actually resolved. This is how we end up with Surface Skimmers and Deflection Masters.

Ignoring Customer Feedback: Traditional scorecards often rely solely on internal evaluators, ignoring what the customer actually thought about the interaction. This disconnect can lead to high QA scores for interactions that left customers frustrated.

Rigid Adherence to Process: While processes are important, scorecards that rigidly enforce them can discourage agents from thinking critically and finding creative solutions to unique problems.

Forced Gratitude: Requiring agents to say "thank you" after every piece of verification information creates an unnatural flow of conversation. It can make the interaction feel robotic and insincere, potentially irritating customers who just want to get their issue resolved.

Let me share another real-world example. I once worked with a credit card company that had a QA scorecard that looked comprehensive on the surface. It had sections for greeting, security, problem-solving, and closing. Sounds good, right?

But when we dug deeper, we found that an agent could get a perfect score without actually solving the customer's problem. The scorecard was great at measuring process adherence but terrible at measuring actual customer satisfaction.

Here's how it broke down:

- Greeting: 10 points for using the customer's name and a scripted welcome.
- Security: 20 points for asking all required security questions in order.
- Problem-solving: 50 points, but this was split into sub-categories like "used proper tools" and "followed troubleshooting steps" rather than "actually solved the problem."
- Closing: 20 points for using a scripted farewell and asking if there was anything else they could help with.

An agent could tick all these boxes, get a perfect score, and still leave the customer with an unresolved issue. Worse, the heavy emphasis on security and closing meant that agents were incentivized to rush through the actual problem-solving to ensure they had time for these scripted elements.

This scorecard was a breeding ground for false hustle. It was creating Checkbox Champions and Script Robots while doing nothing to encourage genuine problem-solving or customer satisfaction.

The Cost of Ignoring False Hustle

Now, I know what some of you might be thinking. "Sure, Tom, this false hustle stuff doesn't sound great, but is it really that big a deal? We're hitting our numbers, after all."

Let me be clear: ignoring false hustle in your contact center is like ignoring a leaky pipe in your house. It might seem like a small problem at first, but before you know it, you're dealing with major water damage and a hefty repair bill.

Here are just a few ways false hustle can cost your business:

1. **Customer Churn**: In today's world, customers have more choices than ever. If they have a bad experience with your contact center, if they feel like they're getting the runaround with scripted responses, they won't think twice about jumping ship to your competitor. And replacing a customer costs a lot more than retaining one. One study by Bain & Company found that increasing customer retention rates by 5% increases profits by 25% to 95%.
2. **Repeat Calls**: When agents are more focused on getting off the phone quickly than on solving the problem, guess what happens? The customer calls back. And again. And again. This drives up your costs and frustrates your customers. The Technical Assistance Research Program found that 54% of customers will call more than once about the same issue if they don't get proper resolution the first time.
3. **Negative Word-of-Mouth**: In the age of social media, one bad customer service experience can quickly become a PR nightmare. False hustle creates exactly the kind

of interactions that customers love to rant about online. According to a study by American Express, Americans tell an average of 15 people about a poor service experience.

4. **Employee Turnover**: Believe it or not, most people who choose customer service as a career actually want to help people. When your processes force them into false hustle, they get frustrated and burn out. High turnover is incredibly costly in terms of both money and institutional knowledge. The Center for American Progress found that the cost of replacing an employee can be anywhere from 16% to 213% of their annual salary.

5. **Missed Opportunities**: Every customer interaction is a chance to upsell, cross-sell, or at least gather valuable customer insights. False hustle rushes through these opportunities, leaving money on the table. A study by Bain & Company found that customers who have the best past experiences spend 140% more compared to those who have the poorest past experiences.

6. **Regulatory Risks**: In many industries, rushed interactions can lead to compliance issues. I've seen companies face hefty fines because their false hustle approach led to mistakes in handling sensitive customer information. For instance, in 2019, a major bank was fined $1.75 million for failing to properly disclose fees to customers, a mistake partly attributed to rushed customer interactions

I once worked with a major retailer a couple years ago at Expivia who was proud of their "efficient" contact center. Their AHT was low, their call volume was high, and their costs were down. On paper, it looked great. The CEO was patting everyone on the back for running such a lean operation.

But when we looked at their customer lifetime value, it was abysmal. Why? Because their false hustle approach was driving customers away in droves.

We did a deep dive into their data and found some alarming trends:

- 40% of customers who contacted the call center made a smaller purchase in the following 6 months compared to their previous shopping patterns.
- 25% of customers who had a call center interaction didn't make any purchase in the following year.
- Their Net Promoter Score had dropped 15 points in the two years since they implemented their "efficiency" measures.

A deeper analysis showed that they were losing millions in potential revenue due to their poor customer service. The money they were saving on their contact center was pennies compared to what they were losing in customer value.

We calculated that their false hustle approach was costing them approximately $30 million per year in lost sales and customer churn. And that's not even counting the long-term brand damage from negative word-of-mouth.

The bottom line is this: false hustle is a silent killer in contact centers. It might make your short-term metrics look good, but it's destroying value in the long run. It's like a sugar high – it feels good for a moment, but the crash is coming, and it's going to hurt.

Conclusion: The First Step to Solving the Problem

As we wrap up this chapter, I want to emphasize one crucial point: recognizing false hustle is the first step to solving it. It's easy to get complacent when your metrics look good on paper. It's easy to assume that if your QA scores are high, your customer service must be great. But as we've seen, that's often not the case.

I want you to take a hard look at your own contact center. Are you seeing signs of false hustle? Are your QA practices inadvertently encouraging it? And most importantly, what might it be costing you in the long run?

Here are some questions to ask yourself:

1. Do your top-performing agents (according to your efficiency metrics) also have the highest customer satisfaction scores?
2. What's your FCR rate? Are customers having to call back multiple times to get their issues resolved?
3. How often do your agents go off-script? Is this encouraged or discouraged?
4. What's your employee turnover rate? Are your agents satisfied with their work?
5. How much emphasis do you place on efficiency metrics vs. customer satisfaction metrics?
6. Do your QA scorecards measure problem resolution, or just process adherence?

Remember, in today's customer-centric business world, addressing false hustle isn't just important – it's essential for survival. Your customers have more choices than ever before, and they're not afraid to use them. One bad experience can lose you a customer for life.

But here's the good news: once you've identified false hustle in your organization, you've taken the first crucial step towards eliminating it. And when you replace false hustle with genuine, effective customer service, the results can be transformative.

In the next chapter, we're going to start talking solutions. We'll look at how to redesign your QA processes, retrain your agents, and create a culture of true hustle that balances efficiency with genuine customer care. We'll explore how to create a contact center that doesn't just look good on paper, but delivers real value to your customers and your business.

Get ready, because we're about to revolutionize your approach to customer service. The days of false hustle are numbered – it's time for the era of genuine, effective, customer-centric service to begin.

3

AI vs. Humans: Why the Future of CX Needs Both Heart and Tech

In the previous chapters, we explored the concept of false hustle and how to identify it in your contact centers. We uncovered the ways in which traditional metrics and approaches can inadvertently encourage behaviors that look good on paper but fail to deliver genuine value to customers. Now, it's time to look ahead and understand why these old approaches are not just ineffective, but potentially disastrous in the rapidly evolving landscape of customer service.

The AI Revolution in Customer Service

We stand at the precipice of a massive shift in the customer service industry. Artificial Intelligence (AI) is no longer a futuristic concept – it's here, and it's rapidly transforming how businesses interact with their customers. Chatbots, virtual assistants, and AI-powered self-service options are becoming increasingly sophisticated, handling a growing percentage of routine customer inquiries with speed and accuracy that would have seemed impossible just a few years ago.

This AI revolution brings both opportunities and challenges. On one hand, it offers the potential for unprecedented efficiency and scalability in customer service operations. On the other, it raises critical questions about the role of human agents and the nature of customer experience in this new landscape.

As AI takes over more routine interactions, the nature of human-handled customer service is changing dramatically. The queries that make it through to human agents are increasingly complex, emotionally charged, or high-stakes. This shift demands a fundamental reevaluation of how we approach customer service, train our agents, and measure success.

The Growing Importance of Human Touch

In this AI-driven world, the value of genuine human interaction is skyrocketing. When a customer reaches out to a human agent, it's often because they've exhausted automated options or because their issue is too nuanced or emotionally sensitive for an AI to handle effectively. These interactions represent critical moments in the customer journey – moments that can make or break a customer's relationship with your brand.

Consider this scenario: A customer has spent time trying to resolve an issue through your website's chatbot and FAQ section. They've become increasingly frustrated as their unique problem doesn't fit neatly into any of the categories your bot is able to handle. By the time they reach a human agent, they're not just looking for a solution – they're seeking understanding, empathy, and reassurance.

In this context, the old metrics of efficiency – average handle time, calls per hour, strict script adherence – are not just inadequate; they're actively harmful. Rushing through these complex interactions or relying on scripted responses is a recipe for customer dissatisfaction and churn.

Instead, we need to prioritize and measure the qualities that make human interaction valuable:

- Emotional Intelligence: The ability to recognize and respond appropriately to the customer's emotional state.
- Problem-Solving Skills: The capacity to think creatively and find solutions to unique, complex issues.
- Adaptability: The flexibility to tailor communication style and approach to each individual customer.
- Deep Knowledge: The expertise to provide insights and information beyond what's readily available online or through AI systems.

The Paradox of Efficiency and Personalization

One of the most challenging aspects of this new reality is balancing the need for efficiency with the demand for personalized, high-touch service. Customers expect quick responses, but they also want their unique needs understood and addressed.

I once worked with a large e-commerce company that prided itself on its efficient customer service. They had implemented a sophisticated ticketing system and set ambitious targets for response times. On paper, it looked impressive, most customer inquiries received a response within minutes.

However, when we dug deeper, we found that these rapid responses were often just the first step in a long, frustrating journey for customers with complex issues. The initial replies were typically generic and didn't address the specifics of the customer's problem. This led to long email chains, repeated explanations from customers, and ultimately, a poor experience despite the "efficient" service.

The lesson here is clear: in complex customer service scenarios, speed without substance is worse than useless – it's actively damaging to customer relationships.

Redefining Value in Customer Interactions

To succeed in this new landscape, we need to radically redefine what we consider valuable in customer interactions. Here are some key shifts we need to make:

- **From Transactions to Relationships:**

Instead of viewing each interaction as a discrete event to be completed as quickly as possible, we need to see it as part of an ongoing relationship with the customer.

- **From Scripts to Conversations:**

Rather than relying on rigid scripts, we need to empower our agents to have genuine, adaptive conversations with customers.

- **From Efficiency to Effectiveness:**

Our primary measure of success should be whether we've truly resolved the customer's issue and improved their relationship with our brand, not how quickly we got them off the phone.

- **From Knowledge Recitation to Knowledge Application:**

In an age where basic information is readily available online, our agents need to be able to apply deep knowledge to solve complex problems, not just recite facts.

- **From Uniform Approaches to Personalized Solutions:**

Every customer and situation is unique. Our approach to service needs to reflect this reality.

The Growing Importance of Emotional Intelligence

Perhaps the most crucial skill for customer service agents in this new landscape is emotional intelligence. As AI handles more routine interactions, human agents are increasingly dealing with customers in emotionally charged situations. The ability to recognize, understand, and respond appropriately to these emotions is becoming a key differentiator in customer service.

41

I witnessed the power of this firsthand while working with a health insurance company. They were facing a crisis of customer confidence, with complaint rates through the roof. Their agents were well-trained in policies and procedures, but they were falling short when it came to handling emotionally sensitive situations.

We tested an emotional intelligence training program, teaching agents how to recognize emotional cues, respond with genuine empathy, and de-escalate tense situations. The results were dramatic – customer satisfaction scores shot up, complaint rates plummeted, and perhaps most tellingly, the agents reported feeling more fulfilled in their work.

This experience underscores a critical point: in the age of AI, our most valuable differentiator is our humanity. Emotionally intelligent service is the antithesis of false hustle. It's about taking the time to truly listen, to connect, and to care.

The Challenge of Measuring What Matters

As we shift our focus to these more nuanced aspects of customer service, we face a significant challenge: how do we measure and encourage these softer skills? How do we evaluate empathy, problem-solving ability, or an agent's capacity to turn a frustrated customer into a loyal advocate?

These are not easy questions to answer, but they are crucial ones. Our traditional metrics and quality assurance processes are simply not equipped to capture these critical elements of modern customer service. In the next chapter, we'll tackle this challenge head-on, reimagining our approach to measuring and encouraging genuine, effective customer service.

Preparing for the Future

As we look to the future, it's clear that the role of human agents in customer service is evolving, not disappearing. While AI will continue to handle an increasing share of routine interactions, human agents will be more important than ever in managing complex, high-value customer relationships.

To prepare for this future, organizations need to:

1. Invest in Emotional Intelligence Training: Equip your agents with the skills to handle emotionally charged situations effectively.
2. Foster a Culture of Continuous Learning: As products and services become more complex, agents need to be constant learners.
3. Empower Agents with Advanced Tools: Provide your team with the technology and information they need to solve complex problems quickly and effectively.
4. Rethink Hiring Practices: Look for candidates with high emotional intelligence, problem-solving skills, and adaptability.
5. Reimagine Quality Assurance: Develop new ways to measure and encourage the skills that truly matter in complex customer interactions.

Conclusion: Embracing the Human Advantage

As we move forward, it's crucial to remember that the rise of AI in customer service isn't a threat to human agents – it's an opportunity. By automating routine tasks, AI frees up human agents to do what they do best: connect, empathize, and solve complex problems.

The organizations that will thrive in this new landscape are those that embrace this shift, investing in the uniquely human skills that AI can't replicate. They're the ones who recognize that while AI can handle transactions, only humans can build true relationships.

In the next chapter, we'll explore how to translate these insights into practical changes in how we measure and manage customer service. We'll reimagine the CX scorecard, creating a new framework that encourages genuine, effective customer service without losing sight of necessary efficiency measures.

The game hasn't just changed - it's become more complex and more human. It's time our approach reflected that complexity, focusing not just on how fast we work, but on how well we serve our customers in an age where human touch is more valuable than ever.ver.

4

Breaking the Busy Cycle: How to Ditch False Hustle for Real Results

In the previous chapter, we explored the critical importance of human interaction in an age where AI is rapidly transforming customer service. We recognized that as AI takes over routine interactions, human agents are increasingly handling complex, emotionally charged, and high-stakes customer issues. This shift demands a fundamental reevaluation of how we approach, deliver, and measure customer service.

Now, it's time to tackle one of the most crucial challenges in this new landscape: how do we measure and encourage the kind of genuine, empathetic, and effective customer service that today's complex interactions demand? Our traditional metrics and quality assurance (QA) processes, designed for a different era, are woefully inadequate for this task. In fact, they often inadvertently encourage the very behaviors we need to eliminate – the false hustle that prioritizes superficial efficiency over meaningful customer outcomes.

The current metrics and QA processes are somewhat outdated. They reward false hustle by prioritizing speed, call duration, and scripted responses over meaningful customer interactions and real problem-solving. In an era where each human interaction is increasingly critical to customer loyalty and brand perception, this approach is not just ineffective – it's actively harmful to your business.

To address this challenge, we need to reimagine our CX scorecard from the ground up. We need to create a new framework that aligns with the realities of customer service in the AI era – one that encourages and rewards the uniquely human skills that make a real difference in complex customer interactions.

This transformation requires a paradigm shift in our thinking. We need to move away from rigid processes and metrics toward understanding customer intent and achieving meaningful outcomes. It's about focusing less on whether the agent followed every step of a script and more on whether the customer left the interaction feeling valued, understood, and with their issue genuinely resolved.

In this chapter, we'll explore the thought process of rethinking the CX scorecard that promotes *genuine service* and combats false hustle. We'll dive into four key elements of this new approach: Empathy, Problem Solving, Call Control, and Communication Skills/Professionalism. For each of these elements, we'll contrast the false hustle approach with a genuine service approach, demonstrating how simple tweaks in evaluation criteria and training can fundamentally reshape how customer service is delivered and measured.

By reimagining our CX scorecard, we're not just changing what we measure – we're redefining what success looks like in customer service. We're creating a framework that prioritizes meaningful, human-centered interactions that foster trust, solve real problems, and drive long-term customer loyalty. This transformation requires a commitment from every level of the organization, but the payoff – happier customers, engaged employees, and stronger business results – is well worth the effort.

Let's begin this journey of transformation, creating a CX scorecard that's fit for the human-AI era of customer service.

The Paradigm Shift: From Scripted Process to Intent and Outcomes

To create a CX scorecard and platform that promotes genuine service, we must start to undergo a profound shift in mindset. The focus needs to move away from rigid processes and metrics toward understanding customer intent and achieving meaningful outcomes.

Traditionally, contact centers have emphasized process adherence: using the "proper" responses, following workflows to the letter, and checking off all the required actions during a call. While this ensures consistency, it often neglects the human element that's critical to effective customer service.

This shift to intent and outcomes involves evaluating how well agents understand and respond to the customer's needs, whether they can solve the problem effectively, and how the interaction contributes to long-term customer satisfaction. It's about focusing less on whether the agent followed every step and more on whether the customer left the interaction feeling valued and their issue resolved.

Transforming Our CX Approach

In our journey to rebuild the CX scorecard, we're going to explore four key elements of the new approach as examples in change: **Empathy, Problem Solving, Call Control,** and **Communication Skills/Professionalism**. These four pillars embody the shift from process-oriented thinking to intent-driven, outcome-focused service.

For each of these elements, we'll contrast the **false hustle approach** (which aligns with the old mindset) with a **genuine service approach** (which embodies the new focus). By breaking down these categories, we can see how simple tweaks in evaluation criteria and training can fundamentally reshape how customer service is delivered.

**** Please note that some of these examples are a little extreme and may seem not as realistic. We did this on purpose to exaggerate the false hustle and make it stand out.

1. Empathy

In the false hustle model, empathy is often reduced to checking off phrases from a script, with agents required to say something like "I understand how you feel" at least twice during a call. But this doesn't translate into genuine connection. In contrast, empathy in the genuine service approach focuses on whether the agent's empathy effectively addresses the customer's emotional needs and improves the interaction.

False Hustle Approach:

"Did the agent use empathy statements like 'I understand how you feel' ?"

Genuine Service Approach:

"Did the agent's empathy response positively influence the outcome of the interaction?"

How This Combats False Hustle:

- **Focuses on the outcome**: Addressing emotional needs and positively influencing the interaction.
- **Implies intent**: Encourages agents to show genuine empathy rather than just reciting canned phrases.
- **Avoids prescriptive actions**: Allows for natural, authentic responses based on the situation.
- **Encourages holistic evaluation**: Evaluators focus on the overall impact of the agent's empathy, not just specific phrases.

Example:

49

- **False Hustle Interaction:**
- Customer: "I've been without internet for three days! This is ridiculous!"
- Agent: "I understand how you feel. I apologize for the inconvenience."

- **Genuine Service Interaction:**
- Customer: "I've been without internet for three days! This is ridiculous!"
- Agent: "Three days? That's not acceptable at all. I can only imagine how frustrating this has been for you. Let's get to the bottom of this right away. Can you walk me through what's been happening?"

Training Implication:

To foster real empathy, agents need more than a set of scripted phrases. We need to teach them to put themselves in the customer's shoes, recognize the emotional impact of issues, and validate the customer's feelings before jumping to problem-solving. This requires developing emotional intelligence and active listening skills.

As you can see, the difference in what is actually being said is really not that different, yet to the customer is huge. Don't you think this is worth 5 more seconds?

2. Problem Solving

In the false hustle approach, problem-solving often boils down to following a troubleshooting script step-by-step, regardless of whether the steps are relevant to the customer's specific issue. True problem-solving involves critical thinking and tailoring solutions to the situation.

False Hustle Approach:

"Did the agent follow the troubleshooting script in the correct order?"

Genuine Service Approach:

"Did the agent apply critical thinking to identify the root cause of the issue and provide a tailored solution?"

How This Combats False Hustle:

- **Promotes thinking over recitation**: Encourages agents to use logic and intuition rather than blindly following a script.
- **Allows creative solutions**: Gives agents the freedom to customize responses based on customer needs.
- **Focuses on resolution**: Evaluates whether the problem was actually solved, rather than whether the process was followed.

Example:

- **False Hustle Interaction:**
- Agent: "Let's try resetting your router. Please unplug it for

51

30 seconds, then plug it back in."
- Customer: "I've already done that three times today."
- Agent: "I understand, but we need to go through all the steps. Let's try it again."

- **Genuine Service Interaction:**
- Agent: "I see you've already reset your router multiple times. That suggests the issue might not be with the router itself. Have you noticed any patterns with the outages? Do they happen at certain times or when using specific devices?"
- Customer: "Now that you mention it, it seems to happen more when my kids are home from school."
- Agent: "That's helpful information. It sounds like we might be dealing with a bandwidth issue rather than a hardware problem. Let's look at your current plan and usage to see if we need to adjust your service to better meet your family's needs."

Training Implication:

Agents must be trained to go beyond surface-level solutions. This requires asking the right questions, digging into customer details, and connecting the dots between seemingly unrelated information. Agents must understand the products they support deeply and have the confidence to make decisions without a rigid script guiding them. using checklists still can be used and probably should be used, as long as we give the agents the bandwidth to use them then right way.

3. Call Control

False Hustle Approach:

"Did the agent adhere to the target handle time?"

Genuine Service Approach:

"Did the agent efficiently address all customer concerns while maintaining a natural conversation flow?"

How This Combats False Hustle:

- **Prioritizes comprehensive problem-solving** over arbitrary time limits.
- **Encourages active listening** and addressing all customer needs.
- **Allows for natural, unrushed conversations** without sacrificing efficiency.
- **Focuses on customer satisfaction** rather than just call metrics like average handle time.

Example:

- **False Hustle Interaction:**
- **Customer:** "Thanks for fixing my internet, but I've been getting way too many marketing emails from your company. Also, I'm thinking about switching cable plans. My neighbor just switched providers, and I don't watch half my channels anyway. Oh, and what's the best streaming service, in your opinion?"
- **Agent:** "I'm sorry, but I can only help with your internet issue. You'll need to contact our billing department for

your other concerns. I can transfer you or you can call back. Anything else about the internet outage specifically?"

- **Customer:** "I guess not."
- **Agent:** "Great! Thanks for calling." *(Ends the call abruptly.)*

- **Genuine Service Interaction:**
- **Customer:** "Thanks for fixing my internet, but I've been getting way too many marketing emails from your company. Also, I'm thinking about switching cable plans. My neighbor just switched providers, and I don't watch half my channels anyway. Oh, and what's the best streaming service, in your opinion?"
- **Agent:** "I'm glad we got your internet working. I can see how those marketing emails could get annoying. I'll help you adjust your email preferences to reduce them. As for your cable plan, our customer service team can help you explore better options. I can transfer you right away or provide the number if you'd prefer to call later. What works best for you?"
- **Customer:** "A transfer would be great!"
- **Agent:** "I'll get you connected. Thanks for bringing this up, and I appreciate your patience today."

Training Implication:

We're teaching agents to manage the flow of the conversation without rushing the customer. The goal is to cover all relevant issues, even those that may seem outside the original scope of the call, while ensuring the customer feels heard and understood. Training should focus on balancing efficiency with comprehensive service, which includes multitasking and active listening.

4. Communication Skills and Professionalism

The false hustle approach to communication often revolves around avoiding errors—making sure agents don't use slang or unprofessional language. While that's important, the genuine service approach focuses on whether agents can clearly communicate, adapt to the customer's communication style, and maintain professionalism while still being personable and effective.

False Hustle Approach:
"Did the agent avoid using slang or inappropriate language?"

Genuine Service Approach:
"Did the agent communicate clearly and professionally, adapting their language and tone to the customer's style while maintaining respect and clarity?"

How This Combats False Hustle:

- **Encourages adaptability**: Allows agents to modify their communication style to meet the needs of the customer while remaining professional.
- **Focuses on clarity and respect**: Ensures that communication is clear, concise, and respectful, with an emphasis

on customer understanding rather than simply avoiding mistakes.

- **Balances professionalism with authenticity**: Encourages agents to be professional but also personable and approachable, avoiding robotic or overly formal interactions.

Example:

- **False Hustle Interaction:**
- Customer: "I'm not very tech-savvy, I'm afraid."
- Agent: "No problem, sir. Please proceed to access your router's configuration page by entering 192.168.1.1 into your browser's address bar. Then navigate to the wireless settings and modify the channel selection."

- **Genuine Service Interaction:**
- Customer: "I'm not very tech-savvy, I'm afraid."
- Agent: "No worries at all, I'm here to help. Let's break this down into simple steps. Think of your router like a radio— it broadcasts on different channels. We just need to change the channel to avoid interference. I'll guide you through each click, and we'll take it slow. How does that sound?"

Training Implication:

Communication skills training should focus not just on avoiding mistakes but on clarity, adaptability, and professionalism. Agents need to be taught how to assess the customer's level of understanding and adjust their explanations accordingly. This means using analogies, asking for feedback to ensure understanding, and maintaining a conversational, yet respectful tone. Role-playing exercises can be particularly effective in honing these skills.

Conclusion: Embracing a New Era of CX

Thinking the the CX scorecard is not just about changing what we measure. It's about fundamentally shifting how we define success in customer service. The new scorecard should prioritize meaningful, human-centered interactions that foster trust, solve real problems, and drive long-term customer loyalty. This transformation requires a commitment from every level of the organization, but the payoff—happier customers, engaged employees, and stronger business results—is worth the effort.

By focusing on intent and outcomes, this new CX approach will not only help combat false hustle but also provide the authentic, effective service that customers crave in today's experience-driven world.

5

Reinventing the Scorecard: Turning CX Metrics into True Service Magic

In our journey to combat false hustle, we've identified its manifestations and understood why it fails in today's customer service landscape. Now, let's examine how we can evolve our evaluation criteria to encourage genuine service. We'll look at common questions found in traditional QA forms and see how we can transform them to promote more authentic, effective customer interactions.

1. Opening the Interaction

False Hustle Approach: "Did the agent use the scripted greeting?"

This encourages robotic adherence to a script, regardless of the customer's state or the context of the interaction.

Genuine Service Evolution: "Did the agent open the interaction in a way that set a positive tone?"

- Did the agent adapt their greeting to the customer's perceived mood or the nature of the interaction?
- Did the opening create a foundation for open, productive communication?

2. Building Rapport

False Hustle Approach: "Did the agent engage the customer by using the customer's name 4 times?"

This arbitrary rule can lead to unnatural, forced use of the customer's name.

Genuine Service Evolution: "Did the agent personalize the interaction and build rapport with the customer?"

- Did the agent use the customer's name in a natural, unforced manner?
- Did the agent find authentic ways to connect with the customer?
- How did the agent's approach contribute to a positive customer experience?

3. Showing Empathy

False Hustle Approach: "Did the agent show empathy by using an empathy statement?"

This can result in insincere, scripted expressions of empathy that customers often find hollow.

Genuine Service Evolution: "Did the agent demonstrate gen-uine understanding and empathy that had a positive outcome with the customer?"

- Did the agent's tone and language align with the customer's emotional state?
- How did the agent's empathy impact the customer's mood and the interaction's outcome?
- Did the agent find authentic ways to acknowledge and address the customer's feelings?

4. Problem-Solving Approach

False Hustle Approach: "Did the agent use the scripted trou-bleshooting guide?"

This can lead to unnecessary steps and frustrated customers if the agent doesn't adapt to the specific situation.

Genuine Service Evolution: "Did the agent properly diagnose and address the customer's issue?"

- Did the agent ask insightful questions to understand the root cause of the problem?
- How well did the agent adapt the troubleshooting process to the customer's specific situation?
- Did the agent explain the reasoning behind their approach, keeping the customer informed and involved?

5. Managing the Interaction

False Hustle Approach: "Did the Agent Control the Call?"

This can lead to agents being overly directive, potentially missing important customer input.

Genuine Service Evolution: "Did the agent guide the interaction while remaining responsive to the customer's needs?"

- Did the agent maintain a clear direction for the interaction without dismissing customer concerns?
- How effectively did the agent balance efficiency with thoroughness?
- Did the agent demonstrate flexibility in their approach when needed?

6. Handling Transfers

False Hustle Approach: "Did the agent transfer when appropriate?"

This doesn't account for whether the transfer was truly necessary or handled in a customer-friendly manner.

Genuine Service Evolution: "If a transfer was necessary, did the agent handle the process appropriately?"

- Did the agent exhaust their own resources before considering a transfer?
- How thoroughly did the agent explain the need for a trans-

fer to the customer?
- Did the agent properly prepare the customer and the receiving department for the transfer?

7. Overcoming Objections

False Hustle Approach: "Did the agent use the proper rebuttal?"

This can lead to agents using canned responses that don't address the customer's specific concerns.

Genuine Service Evolution: "Did the agent address and overcome customer objections or concerns with the correct tool?"

- Did the agent listen to and acknowledge the customer's concerns?
- How well did the agent tailor their response to the specific objection raised?
- Did the agent find a constructive way to move the interaction forward?

8. Cross-Selling

False Hustle Approach: "Did the agent Cross sell when appropriate?"

This can result in forced, irrelevant sales pitches that annoy customers.

Genuine Service Evolution: "If an opportunity for additional products or services arose, did the agent present relevant options to the customer?"

- Did the agent identify a genuine need or opportunity before suggesting additional products/services?
- How well did the agent explain the benefits in terms of the customer's specific situation?
- Did the agent respect the customer's decision if they declined the offer?

9. Etiquette and Professionalism

False Hustle Approach: "Did the agent say please and thank you after all verification info?"

While politeness is important, this rigid approach can feel insincere and robotic.

Genuine Service Evolution: "Did the agent maintain a professional and courteous demeanor throughout the interaction?"

- Did the agent use polite language naturally throughout the conversation?
- How did the agent's tone and word choice contribute to a positive customer experience?
- Did the agent demonstrate respect for the customer's time and situation?

10. Closing the Interaction

False Hustle Approach: "Did the agent use the scripted clos-ing?"

This can lead to abrupt or impersonal endings to interactions.

Genuine Service Evolution: "Did the agent bring the interaction to a satisfactory close ?"

- Did the agent summarize the interaction and any actions taken or planned?
- How well did the agent ensure all the customer's needs were met?
- Did the closing leave the customer feeling positive about the interaction and the company?

Implementing the New Approach

Transitioning to this new evaluation method will require more than just changing the forms. It necessitates a shift in how we train, coach, and develop our agents:

1. Scenario-Based Training: Instead of memorizing scripts, agents should practice adapting to various customer sce-narios.
2. Continuous Feedback: Regular coaching sessions focused on these nuanced criteria can help agents improve their soft skills.
3. Call Analysis Workshops: Team discussions about real call examples can help agents understand how to apply these

principles in practice.

Additional False Hustle vs. Genuine Service Questions

1. Active Listening

False Hustle:

- Did the agent repeat the customer's issue?

Genuine Service:

- Did the agent demonstrate understanding by accurately paraphrasing the customer's concerns?
- Did the agent ask relevant follow-up questions to clarify the customer's needs?

2. Handling Complaints

False Hustle:

- Did the agent follow the standard complaint procedure?

Genuine Service:

- Did the agent allow the customer to fully express their complaint without interruption?
- Did the agent demonstrate empathy and acknowledge the customer's frustration before moving to problem-solving?

3. Product/Service Knowledge

False Hustle:

- Did the agent recite all features of the product/service discussed?

Genuine Service:

- Did the agent focus on the features most relevant to the customer's needs?
- Was the agent able to explain complex features in a way the customer could understand?

4. Time Management

False Hustle:

- Did the agent resolve the issue within the target Average Handling Time (AHT)?

Genuine Service:

- Did the agent effectively balance efficiency with thorough problem resolution?
- Was the customer given adequate time to ask questions and fully understand the solution?

5. Tone and Attitude

False Hustle:

- Did the agent maintain a professional tone throughout the call?

Genuine Service:

- Did the agent's tone convey genuine interest in helping the customer?
- Was the agent able to adapt their tone to match the customer's emotional state appropriately?

6. Proactive Service

False Hustle:

- Did the agent offer additional services from the upsell script?

Genuine Service:

- Did the agent anticipate and address potential future needs based on the customer's situation?
- Were any additional suggestions clearly beneficial to the customer's specific circumstances?

7. Technical Troubleshooting

False Hustle:

- Did the agent follow all steps in the technical support flowchart?

Genuine Service:

- Did the agent show initiative in finding creative solutions when standard procedures didn't work?
- Was the technical explanation tailored to the customer's level of expertise?

8. Customer Education

False Hustle:

- Did the agent provide the customer with the standard product manual or FAQ link?

Genuine Service:

- Did the agent take time to ensure the customer understood how to prevent similar issues in the future?
- Was the educational information provided in a way that empowered the customer?

Conclusion: Fostering Genuine Service

By evolving our evaluation criteria in this way, we're not just changing how we score interactions – we're changing the entire culture of our contact center. We're moving from a mindset of "did the agent follow the script?" to "did the agent create genuine value for the customer?"

This approach discourages the false hustle we identified in earlier chapters and encourages the kind of authentic, adaptive service that today's customers expect. It's not about abandoning structure or efficiency, but about redefining what good service looks like in practice.

In our next chapter, we'll explore specific techniques for putting these principles into action, starting with strategies for calming irate customers. As we move forward, keep in mind how these new evaluation criteria can help reinforce and encourage the behaviors we'll be discussing.

The path from false hustle to genuine service isn't always easy, but with these evolved evaluation criteria, we're taking a significant step in the right direction.

6

Cool Under Pressure: The Art of Calming Angry Customers Like a Pro

In our journey to combat false hustle, we know how crucial genuine, empathetic interactions are, especially when dealing with irate customers. It's in these high pressure situations that the limitations of one size fits all training and scripted responses become glaringly apparent.

This chapter will explore specific techniques for calming irate customers, but first, let's discuss why educating agents on adaptable techniques is far more effective than relying on pre written responses.

The Power of Techniques over Scripted Responses

When we equip our agents with a toolkit of techniques rather than a script, we're empowering them to handle each unique situation effectively. One off scripted responses, no matter how well crafted, often fall short in addressing the nuanced needs of an irate customer. In fact, they can often escalate the situation, making the customer feel unheard and even more frustrated.

Techniques are flexible tools that agents can adapt and apply to a wide range of situations. They allow for genuine, in the moment responses that address the unique needs of each customer. By educating our agents on these techniques, we're providing them with the ability to:

1. Adapt to handle unexpected situations
2. Personalize interactions
3. Think critically to address root causes
4. Manage difficult conversations with confidence
5. Continuously learn and improve their skills

When agents understand the principles behind these techniques, they can apply them naturally and authentically. This approach allows them to handle the situation and calm the customer effectively, rather than rigidly adhering to pre written responses that may not fit the specific circumstances.

By mastering these techniques, agents can transform potentially negative experiences into opportunities for building stronger customer relationships. They'll be able to navigate the complexities of human emotion and communication, turning irate customers into satisfied ones.

In the following sections, we'll explore eight powerful techniques for calming irate customers. Remember, these aren't scripted responses to be memorized, but approaches to be internalized and applied thoughtfully. Each technique offers a different strategy for managing difficult interactions, giving your agents a comprehensive toolkit to draw from in any situation.

Let's dive into these techniques and see how they can revolutionize your approach to handling irate customers.

1. The Empathy + Action Combo

This technique combines genuine empathy with immediate, concrete action.

How it works:

- Express sincere understanding of the customer's frustration
- Immediately follow with a specific, actionable plan to address their concern

Example:

Customer: "I've been overcharged for the last three months and nobody seems to care!"

Agent: "I hear how frustrated you are about these overcharges, Mr. Johnson. I'd be upset too if I were in your shoes. Here's what I'm going to do right now: First, I'm pulling up your account to review the charges. Within the next two minutes, I'll have a full breakdown of where the overcharges occurred. Then, I'll process a refund for the incorrect amounts, which should appear in your account within 3-5 business days. After that, I'll personally review your account settings to ensure this doesn't happen again. Does this plan sound good to you?"

Why it's effective: It validates the customer's feelings while demonstrating immediate action, showing that you're taking their concerns seriously.

Education Method:

What to Listen For: Emotional keywords and tone of voice indicating frustration, anger, or disappointment.

How to Use It: When you hear these emotional cues, immediately acknowledge the emotion, then follow up with a clear, step-by-step action plan. Practice pairing emotional acknowledgments with action statements.

2. The Interruption Buster

This technique helps regain control of the conversation when a customer is too angry to listen.
How it works:

- Allow the customer to express their frustration for 30-60 seconds
- Use the customer's name and a calm, firm tone to interrupt and redirect
- Immediately follow with a question or statement that moves towards problem-solving

Example:
Customer: (Angry, rapid speech for about 45 seconds about poor service and wasted time, basically reading the agent the riot act.)

Agent: "Mr. Johnson. Mr. Johnson, I apologize for interrupting, but I want you to know that I've heard everything you've said, and I understand how frustrating this situation is for you. To make sure I can help you as efficiently as possible, may I ask you a couple of quick questions about your experience?"

Why it's effective: It allows initial venting, then firmly but respectfully redirects the conversation towards resolution.

Education Method:

What to Listen For: Extended periods of uninterrupted customer venting or circular complaints.

How to Use It: After allowing 30-60 seconds of venting, practice using the customer's name firmly but respectfully to interrupt. Follow immediately with a question that redirects the conversation. Role-play various scenarios to perfect timing and tone.

3. The Ownership Approach

This technique involves taking personal responsibility for resolving the customer's issue when they feel like they have been "read the riot act" and ignored multiple times. This multiplies the customer's frustration as now they are no longer focused on the original issue, they are focused on not being helped multiple times
How it works:

- Use "I" statements to take personal responsibility for resolving the issue

74

- Clearly communicate that you will see the issue through to resolution
- Provide specific steps and a timeframe for resolution

Example:

Agent: "Mr. Johnson, **I** want you to know that **I'm** personally taking charge of resolving this issue for you. Here's my plan: First, **I'm** going to thoroughly review your account history over the next 10 minutes. Then, **I'll** consult with our technical team to identify the root cause of the problem. Once we have that information, **I'll** call you back if need be personally with a solution. If for any reason **I** can't reach you, **I'll** leave a detailed voicemail and follow up with an email. You can also reach me directly at this number if you have any questions before then. **My** goal is to have this fully resolved for you by the end of the day. How does that sound?"

Why it's effective: Personal ownership reassures the customer that their issue won't be lost in the system.

Education Method:

What to Listen For: Phrases indicating the customer feels ignored or passed around.

How to Use It: When you hear these cues, immediately take personal responsibility. Practice crafting personalized action plans and communicating them clearly. Role-play scenarios where you commit to specific resolutions within defined timeframes.

4. The Reframing Technique

This technique involves shifting the customer's perspective on the situation.

How it works:

- Listen carefully to the customer's complaint
- Restate their issue, focusing on the core problem that needs solving
- Frame the restatement in a way that points towards potential solutions

Example:

Customer: "Your company is terrible! I've been trying to use this software for weeks and nothing works right. It's all just garbage!"

Agent: "I understand, Mr. Johnson. It sounds like you've been dealing with persistent issues that have prevented you from using our software effectively. Let's break this down: What specific features have you had trouble with? Once we identify those, we can focus on getting each one working correctly for you."

Why it's effective: It demonstrates that you've listened and understood the core issue, moving from general complaints to specific, addressable problems.

Education Method:

What to Listen For: Broad, generalized complaints or emotional outbursts.

How to Use It: Practice restating these general complaints as specific, solvable problems. Conduct exercises where agents transform negative statements into action-oriented questions.

5. The Calm Questioning Method

This technique uses strategic questions to de-escalate the situation and gather necessary information.
How it works:

- Use a calm, measured tone to ask specific, relevant questions
- Keep questions short and focused on gathering key information
- Use the customer's responses to guide the conversation towards solutions

Example:
Agent: "To help me understand the situation better, Mr. Johnson, may I ask you a few quick questions?"

Customer: "Fine, go ahead."

Agent: "Thank you. When did you first notice the issue with your account?"

Customer: "About three weeks ago."

Agent: "I see. And what specifically happened when you tried to log in?"

Customer: "It kept saying my password was incorrect, even though I know it wasn't!"

Agent: "That must have been frustrating. Did you receive any error messages or emails about this?"

Customer: "No, nothing."

Agent: "Alright, thank you for that information. Based on what you've told me, it sounds like we may be dealing with a security feature that was accidentally triggered. Let me check that for you right now."

Why it's effective: Calm questioning can help de-escalate emotional responses and engage the customer's logical thinking.

Education Method:

What to Listen For: Opportunities to gather more information amidst emotional statements.

How to Use It: Develop a list of key questions for common scenarios. Practice asking these questions calmly and strategically to guide the conversation towards problem-solving. Use role-play to perfect the art of interjecting the right questions at the right moment.

6. The Positive Language Pivot

This technique involves reframing negative statements into positive ones.

How it works:

- Listen for negative statements or complaints
- Reframe the issue using positive, solution-oriented language
- Focus on what can be done rather than what can't

Example:

Customer: "Your delivery service is terrible! I've been waiting all day and my package still hasn't arrived!"

Agent: "I appreciate you bringing this to our attention, Mr. Johnson. Let's get your package to you as soon as possible. I can see your package is out for delivery today. I'm going to prioritize your delivery and contact the driver directly to ensure it reaches you within the next two hours. In the meantime, I'll set up text alerts so you'll know exactly when the driver is approaching. This way, you won't have to wait around all day. How does that sound?"

Why it's effective: It shifts the conversation from the problem (late delivery) to the solution (prioritized delivery, direct contact with the driver, and text alerts). It acknowledges the customer's frustration while focusing on positive actions to resolve the issue, helping to defuse anger and create a more constructive interaction.

Education Method:

What to Listen For: Negative statements, complaints, or expressions of dissatisfaction.

How to Use It: Create a 'negative to positive' phrase bank. Practice transforming common complaints into solution-focused statements. Conduct regular drills where agents compete to reframe negative scenarios positively

7. The Educate and Empower Approach

This technique involves providing the customer with information and tools to prevent future issues.
  How it works:

- Explain the cause of the current issue in simple terms
- Provide the customer with information or tools to prevent similar issues
- Empower the customer to take control of their experience

Example: Agent: "Mr. Johnson, now that we've resolved the immediate issue, let me explain why it happened and how you can prevent it in the future. The error occurred because... To avoid this, you can... We also have a self-service tool on our website that allows you to... Would you like me to walk you through how to use it?"

Why it's effective: It transforms a negative experience into a learning opportunity, giving the customer a sense of control and preventing future frustration.

Education Method:

What to Listen For: Expressions of confusion or lack of understanding about products/services.

How to Use It: Develop comprehensive knowledge bases about common issues. Practice explaining complex topics simply. Role-play scenarios where agents must educate customers on preventing future issues.

8. The Gratitude Turn

This technique uses expressed gratitude to shift the emotional tone of the interaction.

How it works:

- Sincerely thank the customer for specific actions or information they've provided
- Explain how their input helps in resolving the issue
- Use gratitude to transition to the next step in problem-solving

Example:

Agent: "Mr. Johnson, I want to thank you for taking the time to explain your situation in detail. The information you've provided is incredibly helpful and will allow me to address your issue more effectively. Your patience as we work through this is also greatly appreciated. Now, based on what you've told me, here's what I propose we do next..."

Why it's effective: Expressing genuine gratitude can disarm anger and create a more collaborative atmosphere.

Education Method:

What to Listen For: Any opportunity to genuinely thank the customer, especially after they've shared information or shown patience.

How to Use It: Practice expressing sincere gratitude in various scenarios. Conduct exercises where agents must find unique aspects to appreciate in challenging customer interactions.

Training Implications: Educating Agents in De-escalation Techniques

Equipping your agents with these de-escalation techniques is not a one-time training event, but a fundamental shift in how we approach customer service education. It requires a comprehensive, ongoing training approach that permeates every aspect of your contact center culture. Here's how to effectively educate your agents and embed these methods into the very DNA of your customer service operation

- **Immersive Scenario Training**

Create a library of realistic, challenging customer scenarios based on actual interactions. Use managers and agents to play the role of irate customers, ensuring a high level of realism.

- **Technique Spotting and Analysis**

Regularly review real customer interactions (calls, chats,

emails) as a team. Have agents identify the techniques used, discuss their effectiveness, and suggest alternative approaches.

Example: Implement a weekly "Technique Spotlight" session where you play a recorded call and pause at key moments. Ask agents, "What technique could be applied here?" and "How might that change the outcome?"

- **Peer Coaching and Mentoring**

Pair experienced agents who excel at de-escalation with those who are still learning. Encourage regular coaching sessions and real-time support during difficult calls.

Example: Implement a "whisper" system where new agents can silently ask for advice from experienced colleagues/managers during live customer interactions.

- **Emotional Intelligence Workshops**

Conduct regular workshops focused on developing emotional intelligence, active listening, and empathy.

- **Real-world Application Challenges**

Create challenges that encourage agents to apply these techniques in their daily lives outside of work.

Example: Launch a monthly challenge like "Use the Reframing Technique in a personal conversation and report back on the results."

· Gamification of Technique Mastery

Develop a points-based system where agents earn badges or levels for successfully applying different techniques.

Example: Create a digital "Technique Mastery" board where agents can see their progress, compete with colleagues, and unlock rewards for reaching new levels of expertise.

· Continuous Feedback Loop

Implement a system for continuous feedback on technique application, both from supervisors and customers.

Example: Use speech analytics software to automatically detect when certain techniques are used in calls, providing immediate feedback to agents and supervisors.

· Crisis Simulation Drills

Regularly conduct surprise drills where agents must handle simulated crisis situations using the techniques they've learned.

Example: Without warning, have actors call in pretending to be extremely irate customers. Reward agents who successfully de-escalate the situation.

· Technique Innovation Workshops

Encourage agents to develop and share their own de-escalation techniques based on their experiences.

Example: Host quarterly "Technique Hackathons" where agents work in teams to develop new approaches to common challenging scenarios.

Remember, the goal isn't for agents to memorize these techniques verbatim, but to internalize the principles and apply them flexibly. By creating a culture of continuous learning and improvement around these de-escalation techniques, you'll equip your team to handle even the most challenging customer interactions with confidence and skill.

Long-Term Education for De-escalation Mastery

Once your agents have grasped the basics of de-escalation techniques, it's crucial to implement ongoing education strategies that reinforce and expand their skills. These long-term approaches will help embed de-escalation techniques into your contact center's DNA:

Advanced Scenario Simulation

Move beyond basic role-playing to create complex, multi-faceted scenarios that challenge even your most experienced agents. Develop a library of intricate customer interactions based on real-life situations.

Example: Create a library of scenarios of each technique done the right way and use these if there is any down time in the center.

Technique Integration Analysis

Evolve from spotting individual techniques to analyzing how agents seamlessly integrate multiple approaches within a single interaction.

Example: In your "Technique Spotlight" sessions, challenge agents to identify not just which techniques were used, but how they were combined for maximum effect. Discuss the nuances of transitioning between techniques mid-conversation.

Real-World De-escalation Case Studies

Move beyond hypothetical scenarios to analyze real-world de-escalation successes and failures from various industries.

Example: Conduct monthly "De-escalation Dissection" sessions where teams analyze high-profile customer service incidents from the news, discussing how they would have handled the situation using their de-escalation techniques.

Customized Technique Refinement

Develop personalized improvement plans for each agent based on their strengths and weaknesses in applying de-escalation techniques.

Example: Look at each agent's interactions to identify their most and least effective techniques. Create tailored learning paths and practice scenarios to address specific areas for improvement.

De-escalation Technique Innovation Incubator

Encourage agents to not just apply existing techniques, but to innovate and develop new approaches.

Example: Launch a "De-escalation Innovation Lab" where agents can propose, test, and refine new techniques. Successful innovations can be incorporated into the official training program.

Multi-Channel De-escalation Mastery

Extend de-escalation training beyond voice calls to encompass all customer interaction channels.

Example: Develop channel-specific de-escalation guidelines and conduct cross-channel simulation exercises where agents must de-escalate a situation that transitions from chat to voice to email.

Customer Feedback Integration Workshops

Regularly incorporate direct customer feedback into your de-escalation training.

Example: Host quarterly "Voice of the Customer" sessions where agents review and discuss customer feedback specifically related to how well escalated situations were handled.

Continuous Improvement Challenges

Create ongoing challenges that push agents to continuously refine and improve their de-escalation skills.

Example: Launch a year-long "De-escalation Master" program where agents work through increasingly difficult challenges, earning certifications and rewards as they progress.

By implementing these long-term education strategies, you'll create a culture of continuous improvement and excellence in de-escalation. This approach ensures that your team doesn't just learn techniques, but truly masters the art of turning difficult customer interactions into positive experiences.

7

Listening Like a Champ: How Hearing Your Customers Can Change the Game

In our journey to combat false hustle, we've explored techniques for calming irate customers and de-escalating tense situations. While these skills are crucial, they're just the beginning. Whether you've just calmed an angry customer or you're handling a routine call, the next critical step is the same: truly listening to the customer.

Active listening is the bedrock of exceptional customer service and the key to avoiding false hustle in our interactions. It's also one of the most challenging skills for agents to master, especially in the high-pressure, high-volume environment of a contact center.

The Challenge of Consistent Active Listening

Let's face it: active listening is hard work. After handling call after call, it's tempting for agents to fall into autopilot mode. They might start to:

- Assume they know the problem before the customer finishes explaining
- Jump to solutions prematurely
- Miss crucial details that make each situation unique
- Fail to pick up on emotional cues that could indicate underlying issues

These shortcuts, born of fatigue and the pressure to handle calls quickly, are classic examples of false hustle. They might seem efficient in the moment, but they often lead to misunderstandings, incomplete resolutions, and even re-escalation of previously calmed situations.

Consider this scenario:

An agent has just spent 15 minutes calming an irate customer who received the wrong product. The customer is now calm and explaining the specifics of their order. The agent, feeling the pressure of their call queue and assuming this is a standard wrong shipment issue, interrupts with a standard return policy spiel. Suddenly, the customer's anger flares up again – it turns out this was a custom order for a time-sensitive event, and a simple return won't solve the problem.

This example illustrates how a lack of active listening can undo all the hard work of de-escalation and turn a potential resolution into a renewed conflict.

The Crucial Role of Active Listening

Active listening goes beyond merely hearing the words a customer says. It involves:

- Fully concentrating on the speaker
- Understanding their message
- Responding thoughtfully
- Remembering key points of the conversation

By mastering this skill, we can tailor our responses to each customer's unique needs and preferences, creating a personalized experience that stands in stark contrast to the one-size-fits-all approach of false hustle.

Ten Techniques for Active Listening

Let's explore ten powerful techniques for active listening and how they can help us create more authentic, effective customer interactions:

Give Your Full Attention: Create a distraction-free environment and focus solely on the customer during interactions. This means minimizing background noise, closing unnecessary computer windows, and mentally setting aside other tasks or concerns. Make a conscious effort to be present in the moment. If you're on a video call, maintain appropriate eye contact to show you're fully engaged.

Use Verbal Affirmations: Employ phrases like "I see," "Uh-huh," and "I understand" to show you're engaged. These verbal cues, also known as minimal encouragers, signal to the customer that you're actively listening without interrupting their flow. Be careful not to overuse them, as this can seem insincere. Vary your responses and use them at natural pauses in the customer's speech.

Ask Clarifying Questions: Use open-ended questions like "Can you tell me more about when you first noticed this issue?" or "How has this problem affected your daily operations?" These questions encourage the customer to provide more detailed information, helping you gain a fuller understanding of their situation. Avoid yes/no questions that can limit the conversation.

Paraphrase and Summarize: Restate key points in your own words to confirm understanding. For example, "So, if I understand correctly, you've been experiencing intermittent service outages since last Tuesday, and it's primarily affecting your email and cloud storage access. Is that right?" This technique not only ensures you've grasped the main issues but also shows the customer you're actively processing what they're saying.

Listen for Underlying Emotions (The best agents can do this!): Pay attention to tone, pace, and word choice to identify emotional cues. A customer might say they're "fine" with a situation, but their tone might indicate frustration or disappointment. Listen for sighs, changes in speaking speed, or emphasis on certain words. Acknowledging these emotions can help build rapport and show empathy.

Use Mirroring: Subtly match the customer's tone, pace, and language style. If the customer speaks slowly and thoughtfully, try to match that pace. If they use more technical language, it may be appropriate to do the same (if you can do so accurately). This technique helps create a sense of connection and understanding. However, be careful not to mimic in a way that could be perceived as mocking.

Avoid Interrupting: Allow the customer to finish their thoughts before responding. Even if you think you know what they're going to say, or you have an immediate solution, resist the urge to cut in. If you need to interrupt for clarification on a critical point, wait for a natural pause and ask politely, "Sorry to interrupt, but could you clarify...?"

Practice Empathetic Listening: Try to understand the customer's perspective and feelings. Put yourself in their shoes and consider how the situation might be affecting them emotionally and practically. Reflect this understanding back to them with statements like, "I can imagine how frustrating this must be for you, especially given the tight deadline you're working with."

Take Notes: Jot down key points during the conversation. This helps you remember important details and shows the customer you value their input. It also allows you to focus on listening without the pressure of remembering every detail. Mention to the customer that you're taking notes to reassure them you're capturing the important points.

Provide a Thoughtful Response: Take a moment to consider your response before speaking. It's okay to have a brief pause to gather your thoughts – this shows you're giving careful consideration to what the customer has said. Your response should address the key points raised by the customer and demonstrate that you've understood both their practical needs and emotional state.

Overcoming the Challenges of Consistent Active Listening

Maintaining active listening throughout a long shift isn't easy. Here are some strategies to help agents stay focused:

- Mindfulness Breaks: Encourage short breaks between calls for agents to reset and refocus.
- Call Variety: If possible, mix up the types of calls agents handle to prevent monotony.
- Active Listening Exercises: Regularly practice active listening skills in team meetings or training sessions.
- Listening Fatigue Management: Recognize that active listening is mentally taxing and implement strategies to combat listening fatigue.
- Continuous Feedback and Coaching: Provide ongoing support to help agents improve their active listening skills.

Remember, developing strong active listening skills is an ongoing process. By implementing these strategies and continuously reinforcing their importance, you can create a culture where active listening is valued and consistently practiced.

Adapting to Customer Needs and Preferences

Active listening isn't just about hearing the customer's words; it's about understanding their unique situation and adapting our approach accordingly. This adaptability is the key to moving beyond false hustle and delivering truly personalized, effective customer service.

Here are four crucial ways to use the information gained through active listening to tailor the customer experience:

- Adjust Your Communication Style: Pay attention to the customer's communication style and mirror it appropriately.
- Respect Time Preferences: Gauge the customer's sense of urgency and adjust your pace accordingly.
- Offer Relevant Solutions: Use the information gathered to propose solutions that truly fit the customer's needs.
- Follow Up Appropriately: Based on the conversation, determine the best method and timing for follow-up

Case Study: The Empathy Revolution at XYZ Tech

(Because of NDA agreements, we cannot talk about the actual names of the customers we have worked with)

XYZ Connect, a mid-sized telecommunications company, was struggling with high customer churn rates and poor satisfaction scores. An analysis of their customer interactions revealed a pervasive culture of false hustle, agents were rushing through calls, adhering rigidly to scripts, and failing to address the emotional needs of their customers. They were bad robots.

The turning point came when they came to use at Expivia to outsource their customer service and have us remake the customer experience, we came up with:

"HEAR": Heightened Empathy and Active Response Initiative

Baseline Assessment:

- Customer Satisfaction (CSAT) score: 65%
- Average Handle Time (AHT): 5 minutes
- First Call Resolution (FCR): 60%

The Empathy Initiative:

- Removed AHT as a key performance indicator
- Introduced the "Empathy + Action Combo" technique (as discussed in Chapter 6) to our outsourced Expivia agents and XYZ Tech's internal agents.
- Implemented bi-weekly empathy training sessions
- Redesigned and educated agent/customer interactions to focus on emotional connection rather than just rigid problem solving steps

Challenges Faced:

- Initial resistance from agents accustomed to prioritizing speed
- Temporary increase in AHT, causing concern among upper

management
- Need for more intensive coaching and monitoring during the transition

Results After 6 Months:

- CSAT increased to 85%
- AHT increased to 6 minutes
- FCR improved to 80%
- Customer churn reduced by 25%

Long-term Impact:

- XYZ Tech became known for its exceptional customer service
- Employee satisfaction increased, leading to lower turnover
- The company saw a 15% increase in customer lifetime value

Key Takeaway: By prioritizing genuine empathy over false hustle, XYZ Tech not only improved its customer satisfaction metrics but also created a more positive work environment and boosted its bottom line.

By implementing these active listening techniques and strategies for overcoming listening challenges, we move far beyond the realm of false hustle. Instead of rushing through interactions or sticking to rigid scripts, we're creating dynamic, personalized experiences for each customer. This approach may require more time and effort in the moment, but it pays dividends in customer satisfaction, loyalty, and long-term business success.

Remember, the goal isn't to handle as many calls as possible in the shortest amount of time if you want to actually improve your CX. The true measure of CX success is how effectively we address each customer's needs and how positive we can make their experience. When we truly listen and adapt to customer needs and preferences, we're not just solving problems, we're building relationships.

This customer-centric approach is the antithesis of false hustle. It requires genuine engagement, critical thinking, and a willingness to go off-script when necessary. It's about seeing each customer as an individual with unique needs, rather than just another ticket to be closed.

As you implement these active listening strategies and techniques for adapting to customer needs, encourage your team to view each interaction as an opportunity to learn about and truly help the customer. Celebrate instances where agents demonstrate exceptional listening skills and go above and beyond to adapt to customer needs. Share success stories where this personalized approach led to outstanding outcomes.

By consistently practicing active listening and adapting to customer needs and preferences, you'll create a customer service experience that stands out in today's automated, often impersonal world. You'll be providing the kind of genuine, human-centered service that no AI can replicate – and that's the ultimate competitive advantage in the age of false hustle.

In our next chapter, we'll explore how to apply these listening and adaptation skills across different industries, recognizing that customer needs and expectations can vary widely depending on the context of the interaction.

8

CX Strategy on Steroids: Customizing for Every Industry

In previous chapters, we've explored the concept of false hustle and its general manifestations in customer service. Now, let's dive into how false hustle appears in contact centers across specific industries and, more importantly, how to identify and combat it. Each sector has its unique challenges and pressures that can lead to false hustle behaviors in contact center operations. By understanding these industry-specific tendencies, we can develop targeted strategies to promote genuine, effective customer service.

1. Healthcare Contact Centers

In healthcare contact centers, agents often deal with sensitive information and anxious patients, which can lead to false hustle practices that prioritize call volume over patient care.

Common False Hustle Practices:

- Rushing through patient inquiries to reduce call times
- Providing generic health advice without considering individual circumstances
- Over-relying on scripts without addressing unique patient concerns

Questions to Identify False Hustle:

1. Did the agent take time to verify the patient's identity and access their full record before providing information?
2. Was the information provided tailored to the patient's specific situation, or was it generic?
3. Did the agent explain medical terms and procedures in a way the patient could understand?

Strategies to Combat False Hustle:

- Implement a "patient-first" approach that prioritizes thorough care over rapid call resolution
- Develop a comprehensive call flow that ensures all relevant patient information is captured and considered
- Train agents to communicate complex medical information in layman's terms
- Encourage agents to escalate complex cases to specialized teams rather than providing rushed, generic responses

2. Financial Services Contact Centers

Financial services contact centers often grapple with the pressure to meet sales targets while providing sound financial advice. This can lead to false hustle practices that prioritize quick sales over client welfare.

Common False Hustle Practices:

- Pushing financial products without fully understanding the client's needs
- Glossing over the risks associated with certain financial services
- Rushing through compliance disclosures to shorten call times

Questions to Identify False Hustle:

1. Did the agent conduct a brief but comprehensive assessment of the client's financial situation and goals?
2. Were all relevant risks and potential downsides clearly explained to the client?
3. Was the recommended financial product or service truly the best fit for the client's needs, or just the easiest to process?

Strategies to Combat False Hustle:

- Implement a "best interest" standard that prioritizes client welfare over sales targets
- Develop a robust needs assessment tool that helps agents

match products to client requirements
- Create a compliance checklist that must be completed and verified for each client interaction
- Reward agents based on customer satisfaction and problem resolution, not just call times or sales numbers

3. Retail Contact Centers

Retail contact centers often face high-volume, fast-paced interactions where the pressure to handle calls quickly can lead to false hustle practices that neglect genuine customer needs.

Common False Hustle Practices:

- Pushing for upsells or cross-sells without considering customer needs
- Providing generic product information instead of tailored recommendations
- Rushing customers through the support process to handle more calls

Questions to Identify False Hustle:

1. Did the agent take the time to understand the customer's specific needs and preferences?
2. Were product recommendations based on the customer's requirements, or just on what's currently on promotion?
3. Was the customer given adequate information to make an informed decision, or pressured into a quick purchase?

Strategies to Combat False Hustle:

- Implement a needs-based support approach that prioritizes customer satisfaction over call volume
- Develop a comprehensive product knowledge database for all agents
- Create a customer feedback system that specifically evaluates the helpfulness and relevance of agent recommendations
- Reward agents based on customer satisfaction scores rather than just call handling times

4. Technology Sector Contact Centers

Tech support contact centers often deal with complex issues and a wide range of user expertise. This can lead to false hustle practices that prioritize quick fixes over comprehensive solutions.

Common False Hustle Practices:

- Providing generic troubleshooting steps without understanding the specific issue
- Using technical jargon to impress rather than inform customers
- Rushing to close tickets without ensuring the problem is fully resolved

Questions to Identify False Hustle:

1. Did the agent take the time to understand the customer's level of technical expertise?
2. Was the explanation of the problem and solution tailored to the customer's level of understanding?
3. Did the agent follow up to ensure the solution actually resolved the customer's issue?

Strategies to Combat False Hustle:

- Develop a "tech translation" program that trains agents to explain complex concepts in simple terms
- Implement a tiered support system that matches customer issues with appropriately skilled agents
- Create a knowledge base that allows agents to quickly access and share detailed, product-specific information
- Establish a follow-up protocol to ensure issues are fully resolved before closing support tickets

5. Hospitality Industry Contact Centers

Hospitality contact centers often face the challenge of maintaining high-quality, personalized service in high-volume environments, which can lead to false hustle practices that prioritize efficiency over guest experience.

Common False Hustle Practices:

- Providing scripted, impersonal responses to guest inquiries
- Rushing guests through booking or reservation processes
- Neglecting to address or follow up on guest complaints promptly

Questions to Identify False Hustle:

1. Did the agent take the time to understand and address the guest's specific needs or preferences?
2. Was the guest's experience personalized, or did it feel like a one-size-fits-all approach?
3. Were any issues or complaints resolved to the guest's satisfaction by the end of the call?

Strategies to Combat False Hustle:

- Implement a guest preference system that allows agents to quickly access and act on individual guest information
- Develop a comprehensive training program focused on cultural sensitivity and personalized service
- Create a robust system for tracking and resolving guest issues, with clear accountability and follow-up procedures
- Reward agents based on guest satisfaction scores and the ability to create positive experiences, not just call metrics

By identifying and addressing these industry-specific false hustle practices in contact centers, organizations can move towards more genuine, effective customer service. Remember, the goal is not just to handle calls quickly, but to provide real value and build lasting relationships with customers across all industries.

In our next chapter, we'll explore how to build a contact center culture that naturally resists false hustle and promotes authentic customer service at every level of the organization.

9

Beyond Numbers: Metrics That Tell the Real Story of Customer Success

In our journey to combat false hustle and promote genuine customer service, we've explored various strategies and techniques. But how do we know if these efforts are truly succeeding? The answer lies in how we measure success. In this chapter, we'll dive deep into the world of customer service metrics, exploring how to move beyond traditional KPIs, develop new metrics for authentic engagement, and strike the right balance between efficiency and quality.

The Problem with Traditional KPIs

Traditional contact center KPIs often focus heavily on efficiency and quantitative measures. While these metrics have their place, an overemphasis on them can inadvertently promote false hustle. Let's examine some common traditional KPIs, their limitations, and how they can be misused:

Average Handle Time (AHT):

- Definition: The average duration of a customer interaction, including talk time, hold time, and after-call work.
- Limitation: Focusing too heavily on AHT can encourage agents to rush through calls, potentially sacrificing quality for speed.
- Example of Misuse: An agent might hurry through a complex customer issue, providing incomplete information or failing to address all concerns, just to keep their AHT low.

Average Speed of Answer (ASA):

- Definition: The average time customers wait in the queue before their call is answered by an agent.
- Limitation: While important for customer satisfaction, focusing too heavily on ASA can lead to rushed greetings or inadequate preparation time for agents between calls.
- Example of Misuse: Agents might answer calls immediately but then put customers on hold while they gather necessary information, leading to a technically good ASA but a poor customer experience.

Service Level Agreement (SLA):

- Definition: The percentage of calls answered within a predetermined time threshold (e.g., 80% of calls answered within 20 seconds).
- Limitation: An overemphasis on meeting SLA targets can pressure agents to rush through calls or cut corners to quickly answer the next call in queue.

- Example of Misuse: Managers might pressure agents to end calls prematurely to answer waiting calls, sacrificing quality for quantity.

Adherence to Schedule:

- Definition: The percentage of time agents are available for customer interactions as scheduled.
- Limitation: While important for staffing, this doesn't reflect the quality of service provided during those times.
- Example of Misuse: Agents might avoid taking necessary breaks or skip important training sessions to maintain high adherence, potentially leading to burnout or knowledge gaps.

The Overinflation of Efficiency Metrics

In many contact centers, there's a tendency to elevate efficiency metrics to a status of supreme importance. This often stems from a well-intentioned desire to manage costs, increase productivity, and serve as many customers as possible. However, this approach can lead to several problems:

1. **Misaligned Incentives**: When agents and managers are primarily evaluated on efficiency metrics, they're incentivized to prioritize speed over quality. This can lead to rushed interactions, incomplete problem resolution, and a lack of empathy - all hallmarks of false hustle.
2. **Customer Dissatisfaction**: While customers appreciate quick service, they value thorough problem resolution and

feeling heard even more. An overemphasis on efficiency can lead to superficial interactions that leave customers feeling undervalued and frustrated.

3. **Increased Repeat Contacts**: When issues aren't fully resolved due to rushed interactions, customers often need to call back, ironically decreasing overall efficiency and increasing costs.

4. **Employee Burnout**: Constant pressure to meet aggressive efficiency targets can lead to stress and burnout among agents, potentially increasing turnover and decreasing service quality.

5. **Missed Opportunities**: An excessive focus on efficiency can cause agents to miss opportunities for building rapport, cross-selling, or gathering valuable customer feedback.

The Proper Place of Efficiency Metrics

It's crucial to understand that efficiency metrics are not inherently bad. In fact, they play a vital role in contact center management:

1. **Resource Planning**: Metrics like AHT and ASA are essential for accurate workforce management and ensuring appropriate staffing levels. For example, understanding your average handle time helps determine how many agents you need during peak hours.

2. **Identifying Process Issues**: Unusual spikes in metrics like AHT can help identify system problems or training needs. If you suddenly see a significant increase in average handle time, it might indicate a system slowdown or a new

process that agents are struggling with.

3. **Setting Baseline Expectations**: Efficiency metrics provide a baseline for reasonable customer and agent expectations. Knowing your average speed of answer, for instance, helps set realistic expectations for customers about wait times.

4. **Cost Management**: These metrics help in managing operational costs, which is crucial for the sustainability of the business. Understanding your efficiency metrics can help identify areas where you might be overstaffed or understaffed, allowing for better resource allocation.

The key is to use these metrics as part of a balanced scorecard, not as the sole measure of success. They should be considered alongside quality and customer satisfaction metrics to get a complete picture of contact center performance.

Moving Beyond Traditional KPIs: Refocusing Questions

As we shift our focus to intent and outcomes, we can repurpose and enhance traditional metrics to provide more meaningful insights into the quality of customer interactions. Here's how we can evolve our approach:

Rethinking NPS and CSAT:

- Traditional Approach: "How likely are you to recommend our company to a friend or colleague?" (NPS)
- Evolved Approach: "Based on your interaction with this agent, how likely are you to hire this agent to work in your service center?" (NPS)

- Traditional Approach: "How satisfied were you with your overall experience?" (CSAT)
- Evolved Approach: "How well did the agent understand and address your concerns?" (CSAT)

These reformulated questions shift the focus from the outcome to the agent's performance and intent. They provide more specific feedback on the quality of the interaction itself.

Sentiment Analysis Scores: Implement advanced speech analytics to analyze tone, word choice, and emotional cues to gauge the true quality of the interaction. This helps understand not just what was said, but how it was said and received. Example: A customer might say they're "fine" with a resolution, but their tone indicates frustration. Sentiment analysis can pick up on these nuances, providing a more accurate picture of the customer's true feelings.

Agent Hiring Potential Score: Ask customers: "On a scale from 1 to 5, with 5 being definitely 'yes,' and 1 being definitely 'no,' how likely would you be to hire the last representative you talked to, if you ran a customer service company?"

This question directly assesses the agent's performance from the customer's perspective, focusing on their skills and approach rather than the outcome. It encourages agents to think about how they're presenting themselves professionally.

Intent-Focused Customer Effort Score (CES): Traditional CES: "How much effort did you personally have to put forth to handle your request?" Evolved CES: "The agent made every effort

113

to simplify the resolution process" (rated on a scale of 1-5). This modification emphasizes the agent's effort and intent to simplify the process, rather than just measuring how easy or difficult the customer found the interaction.

By implementing these evolved metrics, we create a more holistic view of customer service quality that aligns with our focus on genuine interactions and meaningful outcomes. We're not just measuring efficiency or satisfaction, but the depth and quality of the customer experience.

Developing New Metrics for Authentic Engagement

To truly capture genuine customer service, we need to go beyond even the more customer-centric KPIs. Here are some innovative metrics that can help measure authentic engagement:

Implementing and Adapting New Metrics

Introducing new metrics requires careful planning and execution. Here's a step-by-step approach:

Assess Current State:

- Evaluate your existing metrics and identify gaps in measuring genuine customer service.
- Gather feedback from agents, managers, and customers on what they believe constitutes qenuine service.
- Example: Conduct focus groups with top-performing

agents to understand what they believe contributes to positive customer interactions.

Define Objectives:

- Clearly articulate what you want to achieve with new metrics (e.g., improve customer loyalty, increase genuine engagements).
- Align these objectives with overall business goals.
- Example: If your business goal is to increase customer retention, you might focus on metrics that measure the depth of customer relationships, like the Rapport Building Score.

Pilot New Metrics:

- Start with a small-scale implementation of new metrics.
- Run the new metrics alongside existing ones to compare results.
- Example: Implement the new metrics in one team or department for a month, comparing the results to teams still using traditional metrics.

Train and Communicate:

- Educate agents and managers on new metrics and their importance.
- Clearly communicate how performance will be evaluated under the new system.
- Example: Develop a comprehensive training program that includes role-playing exercises to demonstrate how the

new metrics translate into real-world interactions.

Continuously Refine:

- Regularly review the effectiveness of new metrics.
- Be prepared to adjust weightings or introduce new metrics as needed.
- Example: Conduct quarterly reviews of the new metrics, gathering feedback from agents, managers, and customers to identify areas for improvement.

Technology Integration:

- Invest in tools that can help measure and analyze new metrics, such as speech analytics software or advanced CRM systems.
- Example: Implement an AI-powered speech analytics tool that can automatically score calls on metrics like Conversation Flow and Emotional Journey Mapping.

Conclusion

Measuring success in genuine customer service requires a fundamental shift in how we approach contact center metrics. By moving beyond traditional KPIs, developing new metrics for authentic engagement, and carefully balancing efficiency with quality, we can create a measurement framework that truly reflects the value of genuine customer interactions.

Remember, the goal of these metrics is not just to evaluate performance, but to drive behaviors that result in meaningful, satisfying customer experiences. As you implement these new approaches, keep the focus on what truly matters: building strong, lasting relationships with your customers.

In the next chapter, we'll explore how to use these metrics to drive continuous improvement and foster a culture of genuine customer service excellence throughout your organization. We'll look at how to create feedback loops, implement coaching programs, and align incentives to support your new customer-centric approach.

By embracing these new metrics and measurement approaches, you're taking a significant step towards combating false hustle and promoting genuine, effective customer service. It's a journey that requires commitment and continuous refinement, but the rewards – in terms of customer loyalty, employee satisfaction, and business success – are well worth the effort.

10

The Secret Sauce: Hiring and Onboarding Emotionally Intelligent Agents

Hiring and Onboarding Emotionally Intelligent Agents

As we've explored in previous chapters, the key to combating false hustle lies in genuine, empathetic customer interactions. But how do we ensure our frontline agents have the emotional intelligence necessary to deliver this level of service? It starts with hiring the right people and onboarding them effectively. In this chapter, we'll dive deep into strategies for identifying, hiring, and developing emotionally intelligent agents who can naturally resist the pull of false hustle.

The Importance of Emotional Intelligence in Customer Service

Emotional intelligence (EI) is the ability to recognize, understand, and manage our own emotions, as well as recognize, understand and influence the emotions of others. In customer service, this translates to agents who can:

1. Remain calm under pressure
2. Empathize with frustrated customers
3. Adapt their communication style to different personalities
4. Read between the lines to understand underlying customer needs
5. Manage their own stress and avoid burnout

These skills are crucial in avoiding false hustle. An emotionally intelligent agent is less likely to rush through calls or resort to scripted responses. Instead, they'll take the time to truly understand and address the customer's needs.

Let's break down why each of these skills is so vital:

Remaining calm under pressure:

When an agent can stay composed during heated interactions, they're able to think clearly and find solutions, rather than rushing to end the call (a classic false hustle move).

Empathizing with frustrated customers:

This ability allows agents to connect on a human level, which is impossible with false hustle tactics. It turns confrontations into collaborations.

Adapting communication styles:

This flexibility is the antithesis of the one-size-fits-all approach of false hustle. It ensures each customer feels understood and valued.

Reading between the lines:

This skill helps agents address the root cause of issues, not just surface-level symptoms, leading to more satisfying and complete resolutions.

Managing personal stress:

Agents who can regulate their own emotions are less likely to burn out or resort to false hustle tactics when under pressure.

Hiring for Emotional Intelligence

When hiring for customer service roles, it's tempting to focus solely on experience or technical skills. But to truly combat false hustle, we need to prioritize emotional intelligence. Here are some in-depth interview techniques to help identify emotionally intelligent candidates:

Situational Questions:

Present scenarios that require emotional intelligence to handle effectively.

For example:

"Tell me about a time when you had to deal with a particularly angry customer. How did you handle it?"

"Describe a situation where you had to say no to a customer's request. How did you manage their disappointment?"

"Can you share an experience where you turned a negative customer interaction into a positive one?"

Look for answers that demonstrate empathy, problem-solving skills, and the ability to manage both the customer's and their own emotions.

Role-Playing Exercises:

Set up mock customer interactions to see how candidates respond in real-time.

Here are some scenarios to consider:

An irate customer whose order has been delayed for the third time

A confused elderly customer struggling to understand a new technology

A customer who's upset about a recent policy change

During these exercises, pay attention to:

How well the candidate listens and picks up on emotional cues

Their ability to remain calm and professional under pressure

How they adapt their communication style to the "customer's" needs

Their creativity in finding solutions

Emotional Intelligence Assessments:

Consider using validated EI assessment tools as part of your hiring process. While these shouldn't be the sole determining factor, they can provide valuable insights.

Some popular options include:

- The Mayer-Salovey-Caruso Emotional Intelligence Test (MSCEIT)
- The Emotional and Social Competency Inventory (ESCI)
- The Genos Emotional Intelligence Inventory

Remember to use these in conjunction with other hiring methods for a well-rounded view of the candidate.

Behavioral Questions:

Ask questions that reveal how candidates have handled emotional situations in the past.

For instance:

"Describe a situation where you had to deliver bad news to a customer. How did you approach it?"

"Tell me about a time when you had to collaborate with a difficult coworker. How did you manage the relationship?"

"Can you share an experience where you had to motivate a discouraged team member?"

Look for answers that demonstrate self-awareness, empathy, and effective emotional management.

Self-Awareness Probes:

Ask questions that gauge the candidate's level of self-awareness, a key component of emotional intelligence.

For example:

"Can you tell me about a time when you received feedback that was difficult to hear? How did you react, and what did you learn from it?"

"Describe a situation where your initial emotional reaction to something was not appropriate. How did you handle it?"

"What aspects of customer service do you find most challenging emotionally, and how do you manage these challenges?"

These questions can reveal a candidate's capacity for self-reflection and growth, crucial traits for avoiding false hustle mentalities.

Stress Tolerance Assessment:

Include questions or scenarios that assess how candidates handle stress, such as:

"Describe a time when you were under significant pressure at work. How did you cope?"

"If you had five customers waiting and your computer suddenly crashed, what would you do?"

Look for responses that demonstrate resilience, problem-solving under pressure, and the ability to maintain composure in challenging situations.

Remember, the goal isn't to find candidates who never get stressed or upset. It's to find those who can recognize and manage their emotions effectively, even in challenging situations.

Onboarding for Emotional Intelligence

Once you've hired emotionally intelligent agents, the onboarding process is crucial in setting them up for success and reinforcing the importance of genuine customer interactions over false hustle. Here's how to structure an onboarding program that emphasizes emotional intelligence:

Empathy Training:

Start with exercises that help new hires put themselves in the customer's shoes.

This could include:

- Role-playing exercises where new hires play the customer role
- Case studies of both successful and unsuccessful customer interactions
- Having new hires use your product or service as a customer

125

would, including going through the support process

Active Listening Workshops:

Conduct workshops focused on active listening techniques.

This ties directly back to our discussion in Chapter 5 about the importance of truly hearing and understanding the customer.

Include exercises like:

- "Reflection" practice, where one person speaks for a minute and the other must accurately summarize what was said
- "Emotion detection" drills, where participants must identify emotions based on tone of voice or written communication
- "Interruption awareness" exercises to help agents recognize and avoid the urge to interrupt

Stress Management Techniques:

Teach new hires techniques for managing their own stress and emotions.

This could include:

- Mindfulness and meditation exercises
- Breathing techniques for quick stress relief between calls
- Time management strategies to prevent feeling overwhelmed
- Physical wellness tips, like the importance of staying hy-

drated and taking regular breaks

Shadowing and Reverse Shadowing:

Implement a comprehensive shadowing program:

- Have new hires observe experienced agents who excel at emotionally intelligent customer service
- Provide a checklist of EI behaviors to watch for during observations
- After shadowing, have new hires take calls while being observed, with immediate feedback and coaching
- Implement a "whisper" system where experienced agents can provide real-time guidance to new hires during live calls

Continuous Feedback Loop:

Implement a system for ongoing feedback and coaching focused on emotional intelligence:

- Regular review of call recordings, with a focus on emotional intelligence metrics
- Peer feedback sessions where agents can learn from each other's experiences
- Self-reflection exercises, such as journaling about challenging customer interactions
- One-on-one coaching sessions focused on EI skill development
- Use of AI-powered sentiment analysis tools to provide objective feedback on customer interactions

Emotional Intelligence Book Club:

Start a book club focusing on emotional intelligence and customer service excellence.

Some recommended potential titles include:

"Emotional Intelligence 2.0" by Travis Bradberry and Jean Greaves:

This book is a popular guide on how to enhance your emotional intelligence. It offers strategies to improve self-awareness, self-management, social awareness, and relationship management.

"Empathy in Action" by Tony Bates and Natalie Petouhoff:

This book discusses the role of empathy in the workplace, particularly in the context of customer experience and digital transformation. It emphasizes how empathy can drive business success.

11

QA That Matters: Building a Quality Assurance System That Drives Real Results

Comprehensive Call Center Quality Assurance

Throughout this book, we've explored the insidious nature of false hustle in customer service, those empty gestures and superficial actions that give the appearance of good service without actually solving customer problems or building meaningful relationships. Now, it's time to tackle this issue head-on through a comprehensive quality assurance (QA) program that reinforces genuine customer service while ensuring compliance and security.

The Importance of Call Center QA

A well-designed QA program is more than just a scoring system. It's a powerful tool for continuous improvement, agent development, and ultimately, customer satisfaction. However, traditional QA often inadvertently encourages false hustle by focusing on superficial metrics that don't truly reflect the quality of customer interactions.

An effective QA program should:

1. Align with your overall customer service goals
2. Provide actionable feedback for agents
3. Identify trends and areas for improvement
4. Reinforce best practices
5. Celebrate genuine customer connections
6. Ensure compliance with regulatory requirements and company policies

Most importantly, it should actively discourage false hustle by rewarding genuine, effective customer interactions over empty gestures or robotic adherence to scripts.

The Challenge and Importance of Subjective Evaluation

As we reimagine our QA scorecard to combat false hustle, it's crucial to acknowledge a significant shift: many of these evaluation criteria are more subjective and nuanced than traditional, checklist style QA questions.

This subjectivity can make scoring more challenging and time consuming for human QA staff (more on this later :). However, we must remember that just because something is harder doesn't mean it's wrong. In fact, this more nuanced approach is essential for truly evaluating the quality of customer interactions and eliminating false hustle.

Why Subjective Evaluation Matters:

Captures the Essence of Genuine Service:
Authentic customer interactions can't be reduced to a simple yes/no checklist. The warmth of an agent's tone, the sincerity of their empathy, and the creativity of their problem solving are all subjective qualities that make a real difference to customers.

Reflects Real Customer Experiences:
Customers don't evaluate their experiences based on whether an agent ticked all the boxes. They remember how the interaction made them feel, which is inherently subjective.

Encourages Thoughtful Analysis:
Subjective evaluation requires QA specialists to think critically about each interaction, considering context and nuance. This deeper analysis leads to more valuable insights and feedback.

Discourages False Hustle:
Checklist style evaluations can inadvertently encourage false hustle by rewarding superficial actions. Subjective evaluation looks beyond these surface-level behaviors to assess genuine quality.

Reimagining the QA Scorecard: A Comparison

(I know we talk about this as well in chapter 5 but here is a little more exhaustive look at more scenarios)

The heart of any QA program is the scorecard used to evaluate customer interactions. Let's compare a new QA scorecard designed to combat false hustle and promote authentic customer service with an old, checklist-style approach that can inadvertently encourage false hustle.

1. Opening and Greeting

New Approach (Genuine Interactions)

- Did the agent provide a warm, genuine welcome?
- Did the agent's greeting sound natural rather than scripted?
- Did the agent establish a positive tone for the interaction?

What to Listen For:

- Personalized greetings like "Good morning, thanks for calling! How can I brighten your day?"
- Natural voice inflections and pacing, not robotic recitation
- Friendly, upbeat tone that conveys genuine interest

Old Approach (Process-Focused, Potential for False Hustle)

- Did the agent say "Thank you for calling [Company Name], this is [Agent Name]"?
- Did the agent use the customer's name at least once in the first 30 seconds?

- Did the agent offer assistance within the first 15 seconds?

2. Verification and Security

New Approach

- Did the agent explain the need for verification in a customer-friendly manner?
- Did the agent handle sensitive information securely and in compliance with data protection regulations?

What to Listen For:

- Explanations like "To protect your account, I'll need to verify a few details. This helps ensure only you have access to your information."
- Lowered voice when repeating sensitive information
- Guiding customers to more secure verification methods when appropriate

Old Approach

- Did the agent ask for the customer's account number?
- Did the agent verify at least two pieces of identifying information?

3. Issue Identification and Empathy

New Approach

- Did the agent ask thoughtful, probing questions to understand the customer's issue?
- Did the agent actively listen and validate the customer's concerns?
- Did the agent respond to the customer's emotional state with genuine understanding?

What to Listen For:

- Open-ended questions like "Can you walk me through what happened?"
- Reflective statements such as "It sounds like this has been really frustrating for you"
- Empathetic responses like "I can understand why you'd feel that way. Let's see how we can turn this around for you"

Old Approach

- Did the agent ask "How may I assist you today?"
- Did the agent restate the customer's issue?
- Did the agent say "I understand" or "I apologize" at least once?

4. Call Control and Navigation

New Approach

- Did the agent guide the conversation purposefully towards resolution?
- Did the agent use silence and hold times strategically and respectfully?
- Did the agent maintain an appropriate pace, neither rushing nor unnecessarily prolonging the interaction?

What to Listen For:

- Clear transitions like "Now that I understand the issue, let's look at some solutions"
- Explaining hold times: "I'll need about two minutes to review your account history. Is that okay?"
- Checking in with the customer: "I want to make sure I'm not going too fast. Do you have any questions so far?"

Old Approach

- Did the agent follow the call flow script?
- Did the agent's hold time not exceed 2 minutes?
- Did the agent resolve the issue within the target handle time?

5. Problem Solving and Resolution

New Approach

- Did the agent offer solutions tailored to the customer's specific situation?
- Did the agent demonstrate creativity in finding solutions, rather than rigidly adhering to standard processes?

What to Listen For:

- Personalized solutions: "Based on your usage patterns, I think this plan would work better for you"
- Creative problem-solving: "That's an unusual situation. Let me check with our product team to see if we can make a custom adjustment for you"

Old Approach

- Did the agent offer a solution from the approved list?
- Did the agent follow the troubleshooting steps in the correct order?

6. Sales and Value-Add Opportunities

New Approach

- Did the agent identify genuine opportunities to add value for the customer?
- Did the agent explain the benefits of products/services in relation to the customer's specific needs?

What to Listen For:

- Contextual recommendations: "Since you mentioned you travel frequently, our international plan might save you money"
- Benefit-focused explanations: "This feature would allow you to do X, which sounds like it would address the concern you mentioned earlier"

Old Approach

- Did the agent attempt to upsell or cross-sell?
- Did the agent mention at least two product features?

7. Call Closing

New Approach

- Did the agent ensure all the customer's concerns were addressed?
- Did the agent end the call on a positive note, reinforcing the customer relationship?

What to Listen For:

- Open-ended checkpoints: "Before we wrap up, what other questions can I answer for you?"
- Positive reinforcement: "I'm glad we could get this sorted out for you today. Please don't hesitate to reach out if you need anything else"

Old Approach

- Did the agent ask "Is there anything else I can help you with today?"
- Did the agent thank the customer for their business?

8. Overall Quality and Compliance

New Approach

- Did the agent maintain a genuine, conversational tone throughout the interaction?
- Did the agent balance company requirements with authentic customer service?

What to Listen For:

- Natural conversation flow with appropriate give-and-take
- Seamlessly incorporating required elements without disrupting the conversation
- Adapting language and tone to match the customer's style

Old Approach

- Did the agent use the required scripted phrases?
- Did the agent avoid using any unapproved language?

Implementing Your QA Process

After refining your QA scorecard to effectively identify and address false hustle, the next crucial step is to implement a comprehensive QA process that ensures the scorecard's potential is fully realized.

Here's how to build a QA process that not only reinforces genuine, effective service but also drives continuous improvement across your team:

Consistent and Targeted Evaluation

Strategic Frequency: Regularly assess interactions to provide timely, actionable feedback. Strike a balance between frequency and workload evaluating 5-10 interactions per agent monthly (if using human scoring) can offer enough insight without overwhelming your team.

Focused Assessments: Tailor evaluations to focus on the most impactful aspects of service. By honing in on specific behaviors or outcomes highlighted in your scorecard, you can ensure that every evaluation drives meaningful improvement.

Rigorous Calibration Sessions

Unified Standards: Regularly conduct calibration sessions with your QA team to align on scoring standards and interpretation of your scorecard criteria. This ensures that all evaluators are on the same page, which is essential for fairness, accuracy, and the identification of true performance trends.

Collaborative Learning: Use these sessions as opportunities for continuous learning and process refinement, encouraging open dialogue about scoring challenges and ambiguities.

Empowering Agent Involvement

Self-Evaluation: Encourage agents to periodically review and score their own interactions. This practice fosters self-awareness and personal accountability, often leading to improvements even before formal feedback is given.

Peer Reviews: Introduce a peer review system where agents can evaluate each other's interactions. This not only provides fresh perspectives but also promotes a culture of collaborative learning and mutual support within your team.

Building Continuous Improvement Loops

Feedback-Driven Training: Use the insights gained from QA evaluations to inform and tailor your training programs. Focus on the specific areas where agents need the most support, ensuring that training is both relevant and effective.

Process Optimization: Analyze QA data to identify inefficiencies or obstacles within your processes that may be contributing to false hustle. This can lead to systemic improvements that enhance overall service quality and agent performance.

By following these steps, your QA process will do more than just enforce standards, it will become a powerful engine for cultural change, driving your organization towards a future where genuine service is the norm and false hustle is a thing of the past

Beyond Scoring: Using QA to Drive Cultural Change

While scoring is an important aspect of Quality Assurance (QA), its true value lies in how you leverage that data to drive meaningful change within your organization. A well-implemented QA process should go beyond simply assigning scores—it should foster a culture where genuine customer service is the norm, and false hustle is systematically eliminated. Here's how to use QA as a tool for cultural transformation:

1. Celebrate Success
    Recognition: QA shouldn't just be about identifying areas

for improvement; it's also about recognizing and celebrating the agents who consistently deliver high-quality, genuine customer service. When agents are acknowledged for their efforts, it reinforces the behaviors you want to see more of. Celebrating success publicly within the organization can also motivate other agents to strive for similar levels of performance.

- **Example:** If an agent receives consistently high marks for empathy and problem-solving, acknowledge their performance in team meetings or through internal recognition programs. This creates a positive feedback loop that encourages other agents to prioritize these behaviors.

2. *Targeted Coaching*

Personalized Development: QA data provides detailed insights into where each agent excels and where they might need additional support. By using this data for personalized coaching, you can help agents improve in specific areas that matter most, such as genuine customer engagement or efficient problem resolution.

- **Example:** If an agent struggles with active listening, use specific call recordings to demonstrate how missed cues led to unresolved issues. Then, coach them on techniques to improve their listening skills, such as paraphrasing or asking clarifying questions.

3. *Team Trend Analysis*

Systemic Improvement: QA data can also be analyzed at the team or department level to identify trends that might point to broader systemic issues. If multiple agents are consistently missing the mark in a particular area, it could indicate that the issue is not with the agents themselves, but with the training, processes, or tools they are provided.

- **Example:** If several agents are rushing through calls without fully resolving customer issues, it might be time to review whether current metrics, like Average Handle Time (AHT), are inadvertently promoting false hustle. Adjusting these metrics could lead to more meaningful interactions and better customer satisfaction.

4. Process Improvement

Efficiency Gains: Use QA insights to refine processes that might be hindering genuine customer service or, worse, encouraging false hustle. When QA reveals consistent issues across multiple agents, it's a sign that something in the process may need to change.

- **Example:** If QA reveals that agents are frequently placing customers on hold to search for information, this could indicate a problem with the knowledge management system. Streamlining access to information can help agents provide quicker, more accurate responses, reducing the temptation to rush through calls.

5. Technology Enhancements

Tool Optimization: QA data can also inform decisions about technology investments. For example, if QA shows that agents are struggling to find answers or are frequently transferring calls due to system limitations, this could highlight the need for better tools.

- **Example:** If agents are consistently receiving low scores for call transfers, it might suggest that the CRM system isn't providing the necessary customer information up-front. Investing in a more intuitive or integrated system could reduce the need for transfers, enhancing both agent efficiency and customer satisfaction.

6. Customer Journey Mapping

Service Optimization: QA insights should inform and refine your customer journey maps, ensuring that every touchpoint is optimized for genuine, effective service. By understanding where customers frequently encounter issues, you can make targeted improvements that enhance the overall customer experience.

- **Example:** If QA data shows that customers are often frustrated during billing inquiries, it might indicate a need to simplify billing statements or improve the training agents receive on handling these inquiries. Adjusting the customer journey at this stage can lead to smoother interactions and higher satisfaction.

7. Compliance Training

Maintaining Standards: Finally, QA data can help ensure that your compliance training is effective. If agents are frequently missing compliance-related QA points, this could indicate a need for additional training or process adjustments.

- **Example:** If QA results show that agents are struggling with compliance scripts, rather than penalizing them, it might be more effective to revisit the training materials or the script itself. The goal should be to ensure compliance without sacrificing the natural flow of conversation.

8. Integrating De-escalation Techniques for Irate Customers

Effective Conflict Management: Dealing with irate customers is one of the most challenging aspects of customer service, and it's crucial that agents are equipped with the right tools and techniques. By incorporating de-escalation techniques into your QA process, you can ensure that agents are not only assessed on their ability to handle difficult situations but also provided with the guidance needed to improve these interactions.

- **Example:** Techniques like the Empathy + Action Combo, where the agent shows understanding and immediately follows up with actionable steps, can be crucial in calming irate customers. Another technique, the Ownership Approach, where the agent takes personal responsibility for resolving the issue, can turn a potentially negative interaction into a positive experience. Use QA data to identify which agents excel at these techniques and which may need additional training.

Case Study 2: "Redefining Quality at GlobalBank"

(We are using the name "Global Bank" as the fictitious name of an actual Expivia financial services customer.)

GlobalBank, a multinational financial institution, was grappling with a disconnect between its quality assurance scores and actual customer satisfaction. Despite agents consistently scoring high on traditional QA metrics, customer complaints were on the rise, particularly regarding the lack of personalized service.

This was the task we were asked to fix at Expivia when Global starting outsourcing with us:

Initial Situation:

- QA scores averaged 92% across all agents
- Customer Satisfaction (CSAT) score: 70%
- High number of repeat calls and escalations
- Agents felt demotivated despite high QA scores

The QA Revolution:

- Redesigned the QA scorecard to focus on outcome and customer sentiment rather than script adherence
- Introduced subjective evaluation criteria, such as "Did the agent provide a warm, genuine welcome?" and "Did the agent offer solutions tailored to the customer's specific situation?"
- Implemented AI-powered Auto QA to analyze 100% of calls
- Introduced peer reviews and self-evaluations

Challenges Encountered:

- Initial drop in QA scores caused concern among agents and management
- Need for extensive training of QA specialists in the new, more nuanced evaluation methods

- Resistance from some long time employees accustomed to the old system

Results After One Year:

- Overall QA scores initially dropped to an average of 83% but gradually improved to 88%
- CSAT increased to 88%
- Repeat calls decreased by 30%
- Escalations reduced by 40%
- Agent satisfaction with the QA process improved by 50%

Long-term Impact:

- GlobalBank's contact center became a model for others in the financial industry
- The bank saw a significant increase in customer retention and cross-selling success
- The new QA process revealed insights that led to improvements in products and services

Key Takeaway: By shifting from a rigid, checklist-based QA process to one that valued genuine customer interactions, GlobalBank was able to align its internal quality metrics with actual customer satisfaction, leading to improvements across the board.

The Broader Impact: Fostering a Culture of Genuine Service

Remember, the ultimate goal of QA is not just to catch mistakes but to foster a culture where genuine, effective customer service thrives, and false hustle is systematically eliminated. By creating an environment where agents feel empowered to be authentic while delivering exceptional service, you can maintain high standards and drive lasting improvements.

12

AI + Agents = Magic: How Technology Can Empower Your Human Talent

Granted, I don't write too much about technology in my books as it is changing so fast and it tends to date my work. Still, I don't think there's much getting around that with all the tech that is coming out and will be changing how we do things. If you're reading this book and it's 2030, these things will probably seem pretty obsolete and funny. Still, I think it's important to talk about these things so we can get to that point.

In our journey to combat false hustle and promote genuine customer service, we've explored innovative metrics that focus on the human element of customer interactions. Now, let's examine how Agent-based AI can enhance these efforts, empowering human agents to provide superior service without losing the crucial human touch.

The rise of AI in customer service has been met with both excitement and trepidation. On one hand, it promises increased efficiency and consistency; on the other, it raises concerns about the depersonalization of customer interactions. However, when implemented thoughtfully, Agent-based AI can be a powerful ally in our fight against false hustle.

It's important to note that technology in this field is rapidly evolving. If you're reading this book in 2030 or beyond, some of these specific technologies might seem outdated. However, the principles behind their use – enhancing human capabilities rather than replacing them – will likely remain relevant.

How Agent-Based AI Combats False Hustle

Agent-based AI tools, when used correctly, can alleviate many of the pressures that lead to false hustle. By providing real-time support, these tools can help agents focus on what truly matters - connecting with the customer and providing meaningful solutions. Here's how:

Reducing Cognitive Load:

- AI can handle information retrieval and routine tasks, allowing agents to focus their mental energy on understanding and addressing the customer's needs.
- Example: Instead of memorizing product details, agents can rely on AI to instantly surface relevant information, freeing them to focus on the customer's specific situation.

Enhancing Decision Making:

- With AI-powered insights and recommendations, agents can make more informed decisions quickly, reducing the temptation to rush or provide generic responses.
- Example: AI can analyze a customer's history and current issue to suggest the most effective solution, helping even new agents perform like seasoned experts.

Improving Consistency:

- AI can help ensure that every customer receives a high standard of service, regardless of the agent's experience level or the complexity of the issue.
- Example: AI can guide agents through complex processes, ensuring all necessary steps are followed consistently across interactions.

Enabling Personalization at Scale:

- By providing relevant customer information and context, AI allows agents to offer personalized service efficiently, even in high-volume environments.
- Example: AI can instantly summarize a customer's history, preferences, and past issues, allowing agents to tailor their approach from the start of each interaction.

Facilitating Continuous Learning:

- AI tools can provide immediate feedback and learning opportunities, helping agents improve their skills in real-time.
- Example: After each call, AI can offer suggestions for

improvement based on the specific interaction, creating a continuous learning loop.

By leveraging these capabilities, we can create an environment where efficiency and genuine customer care are not at odds, but work in harmony. Agents are empowered to provide thoughtful, personalized service, while AI handles the heavy lifting of information management and routine tasks.

Key Areas of Impact

In this chapter, we'll explore three key areas where Agent-based AI can make a significant impact:

1. Agent Assist
2. Real-Time Sentiment Reporting
3. Auto-Summarization

1. Agent Assist: AI as a Real-Time Support System

Agent Assist technology uses AI to provide real-time support to human agents during customer interactions. Here's how it can be leveraged:

a) Intelligent Knowledge Base

- What it does: Surfaces relevant information based on the ongoing conversation.
- How it helps: Agents can quickly access accurate information, improving their knowledge expansion metric and solution creativity index.
- Implementation consideration: Ensure the knowledge base

is regularly updated and that the AI is trained on the latest information.

- Potential challenge: Information overload. The AI needs to be fine-tuned to provide only the most relevant information.

b) Guided Workflows

- What it does: Provides step-by-step guidance for complex processes.
- How it helps: Ensures consistency in service delivery while allowing agents to focus on the customer rather than remembering procedural details.
- Implementation consideration: Workflows should be flexible enough to allow for unique customer situations.
- Potential challenge: Over-reliance on guided workflows could lead to robotic interactions. Agents need to be trained to use them as a guide, not a script.

c) Next-Best-Action Recommendations

- What it does: Suggests the most appropriate next steps based on the conversation context and customer history.
- How it helps: Enables agents to be more proactive, potentially improving their proactive service index.
- Implementation consideration: The AI should be trained on successful past interactions to inform its recommendations.
- Potential challenge: Ensuring recommendations are genuinely helpful and not just upsell opportunities.

153

2. Real-Time Sentiment Reporting: Emotional Intelligence Amplified

Real-time sentiment analysis can provide agents with immediate insights into the customer's emotional state, helping them adjust their approach accordingly:

a) Emotion Detection

- What it does: Analyzes customer's tone, word choice, and speech patterns to detect emotions.
- How it helps: Allows agents to respond with appropriate empathy, potentially improving their empathy score and rapport building score.
- Implementation consideration: The AI should be trained on a diverse range of voices and speech patterns to ensure accuracy across different demographics.
- Potential challenge: Ensuring the AI can accurately detect subtle emotional cues and cultural nuances.

b) Conversation Flow Analysis

- What it does: Monitors the back-and-forth of the conversation, flagging potential issues.
- How it helps: Agents can address communication breakdowns quickly, potentially improving their conversation flow score.
- Implementation consideration: The AI should be trained to recognize different conversation styles and cultural communication norms.
- Potential challenge: Balancing the need for natural conversation flow with the insights provided by the AI.

3. Auto-Summarization: Enhancing Efficiency and Accuracy

Auto-summarization tools can significantly reduce the time agents spend on after-call work while improving the accuracy and consistency of call documentation:

a) **Key Point Extraction**

- What it does: Automatically identifies and extracts the main points of the conversation.
- How it helps: Ensures important details are captured consistently, potentially improving the problem-solving effectiveness metric.
- Implementation consideration: The AI should be trained to recognize industry-specific terminology and key issues.
- Potential challenge: Ensuring the AI doesn't miss nuanced or implied information that a human might catch.

b) **Action Item Identification**

- What it does: Highlights actions promised or required as a result of the interaction.
- How it helps: Ensures follow-up items are clearly documented, potentially improving the proactive service index.
- Implementation consideration: Integrate with task management systems to automatically create follow-up tasks.
- Potential challenge: Distinguishing between firm commitments and casual mentions of potential actions.

c) **Customer Profile Updating**

- What it does: Automatically updates the customer's profile with relevant new information from the interaction.

- How it helps: Ensures customer information is always current, potentially improving the customer relationship index.
- Implementation consideration: Implement a review process to ensure accuracy of automated updates.
- Potential challenge: Balancing the need for comprehensive profiles with data privacy concerns.

Implementation Strategies

To successfully implement Agent-based AI:

1. Start with a pilot program in a specific department or for a specific type of interaction.
2. Provide comprehensive training to agents on how to effectively use the AI tools.
3. Continuously gather feedback from agents and customers to refine the AI systems.
4. Regularly review and update the AI's knowledge base and decision-making criteria.
5. Maintain a balance between AI assistance and human judgment. The AI should enhance, not replace, human decision-making.

Ethical Considerations

As we implement these technologies, we must be mindful of ethical considerations:

1. Data Privacy: Ensure all AI systems comply with data

protection regulations.

2. Transparency: Be clear with customers about when and how AI is being used in their interactions.
3. Bias: Regularly audit AI systems for potential biases in their decision-making processes.
4. Human Oversight: Maintain human oversight of AI systems to catch and correct any errors or inappropriate recommendations.

Conclusion: The Bridge to Auto QA

While we'll dive deeper into Automated Quality Assurance in the next chapter, it's worth noting how these Agent-based AI tools lay the groundwork for more comprehensive quality monitoring. By implementing these technologies, we're not just improving individual interactions, but setting the stage for a more holistic, AI-enhanced approach to ensuring consistent, high-quality customer service.

Remember, the goal is not to automate customer service, but to enhance it. The human touch - empathy, critical thinking, and emotional intelligence - remains at the core of exceptional customer service. Agent-based AI is a tool to amplify these human qualities, not replace them.

As we move forward, it's crucial to maintain a balance between technological efficiency and genuine human connection. By thoughtfully implementing Agent-based AI, we can create a customer service environment that combats false hustle, empowers agents, and ultimately delivers the kind of authentic, effective service that builds lasting customer relationships.

13

From Manual to Magical: The Evolution of AI-Powered Call Center QA

The Evolution of Call Center QA: AI-Powered Automated Quality Assurance

As we've progressed through this book, we've established the critical importance of a robust Quality Assurance (QA) process that prioritizes genuine customer service and eliminates false hustle. Now, let's explore how AI-Driven Automated Quality Assurance (Auto QA) is revolutionizing the way we evaluate and enhance customer interactions at scale, with a particular focus on its ability to score interactions at a much deeper level than traditional methods.

The Technology Behind Auto QA

At its core, Auto QA leverages advanced artificial intelligence and machine learning algorithms to analyze and score customer interactions. This technology, exemplified by platforms like our OttoQA, goes far beyond simple keyword matching or script adherence checks. Instead, it employs sophisticated natural language processing (NLP) and contextual analysis to understand the nuances of human communication.

Key technological components include:

1. **Natural Language Understanding (NLU)**: Parsing and interpreting the meaning and intent behind customer and agent statements.
2. **Contextual Analysis**: Understanding the broader context of the conversation, including industry-specific terminology and situations.
3. **Sentiment Analysis**: Detecting emotional tones and changes throughout the interaction.
4. **Advanced Prompting**: Continuously improving scoring accuracy based on new data and identified patterns.

Scoring at a Deeper Level: Beyond Surface Metrics

The true power of Auto QA lies in its ability to analyze interactions at a depth that would be impossible for human evaluators (the best antidote for false hustle). While human QA specialists often focus on surface-level metrics or specific phrases, Auto QA can delve into the intent, context, and outcomes of interactions. Let's explore this using empathy as a key example.

Empathy Scoring: Human vs. Auto QA

Traditional human scoring of empathy often relies on identifying specific phrases or words, such as "I understand how you feel" or "I'm sorry to hear that." While these can be indicators of empathy, they don't always reflect genuine understanding or positive outcomes.

Auto QA, on the other hand, can analyze empathy at a much deeper level:

1. **Intent Analysis**: Auto QA can examine the context in which empathetic statements are made. It doesn't just look for the presence of certain phrases, but analyzes whether they were used appropriately given the customer's situation.
2. **Response Appropriateness**: The system can evaluate whether the agent's response was suitable for the customer's expressed emotion. For example, if a customer expresses frustration, did the agent acknowledge this frustration before moving to problem-solving?
3. **Emotional Journey Mapping**: Auto QA can track the emotional trajectory of the conversation. Did the agent's empathetic responses positively influence the customer's emotional state over the course of the interaction?
4. **Outcome Correlation**: Most importantly, Auto QA can correlate empathetic behaviors with interaction outcomes. Did expressions of empathy lead to improved customer satisfaction or problem resolution?

Example: Human QA might score an interaction positively if an agent says, "I'm sorry to hear about your issue." Auto QA, however, would go further:

- It would analyze whether this statement was made in response to a specific customer concern.
- It would examine if the agent followed up with questions or statements that demonstrated true understanding of the customer's situation.
- It would assess if this empathetic approach led to a more positive outcome, such as the customer expressing relief or satisfaction later in the call.

Scaling Deep Analysis Across All Interactions

One of the most significant advantages of Auto QA is its ability to perform this deep-level analysis on every single customer interaction. This comprehensive coverage ensures a truly representative picture of service quality across the entire organization.

For instance, OttoQA can analyze thousands of interactions simultaneously, applying the same rigorous, nuanced criteria to each one. This eliminates the sampling bias inherent in manual QA processes and provides insights that would be impossible to gain from evaluating only a small percentage of calls.

Uncovering Patterns and Trends

By analyzing all interactions at this deep level, Auto QA can uncover patterns and trends that would be invisible to human evaluators:

1. **Identifying Successful Empathy Techniques**: The system can pinpoint specific approaches or phrases that

consistently lead to positive outcomes across numerous interactions.

2. **Recognizing False Hustle Patterns**: Auto QA can detect recurring behaviors that indicate false hustle, such as using empathetic phrases without actually addressing customer concerns.

3. **Contextual Performance Insights**: The system can provide insights into how agents perform in different contexts. For example, it might reveal that certain agents excel at empathy in high-stress situations but struggle in more routine interactions.

Customization for Genuine Service Evaluation

Advanced Auto QA platforms allow for significant customization to align with each organization's unique definition of genuine service. For example, OttoQA enables companies to define their own criteria for empathy and other aspects of genuine service, ensuring that the AI's assessments align with the organization's specific values and objectives.

This flexibility allows organizations to move beyond generic service standards and evaluate interactions based on their unique understanding of what constitutes truly excellent, genuine customer service.

Case Study: SmartMart's Auto QA Revolution

Background: SmartMart, a large retailer with over 5,000 agents across 10 call centers, was struggling with inconsistent service quality and a persistent culture of false hustle. Their manual QA process could only evaluate 2% of calls, leading to incomplete insights and delayed feedback.

Challenge: To improve service quality, eliminate false hustle, and create a more consistent customer experience across all interactions without significantly increasing QA costs.

Solution: SmartMart implemented OttoQA, an AI-powered Auto QA system designed to evaluate 100% of customer interactions based on a comprehensive scorecard that included metrics for genuine service and false hustle identification.
Implementation:

1. Scorecard Development: Created a detailed QA scorecard incorporating traditional metrics and new criteria for measuring genuine service, with a particular focus on empathy and problem-solving effectiveness.
2. AI Calibration: Trained the OttoQA system using hundreds of pre-scored interactions to recognize nuances in genuine service and false hustle behaviors.
3. Agent Education: Conducted extensive training sessions to help agents understand the new evaluation criteria and the importance of genuine service over false hustle.
4. Phased Rollout: Implemented the system gradually, starting with a pilot program in one call center before expanding company-wide.
5. Continuous Refinement: Regularly updated the AI models based on feedback from QA specialists and evolving service standards.

Results: After one months of full implementation:

- Evaluation Coverage: Increased from 2% to 50% of all customer interactions.
- Empathy Analysis: OttoQA identified that agents who expressed empathy early in calls and followed up with concrete actions had 45% higher customer satisfaction scores.
- False Hustle Reduction: Instances of identified false hustle behaviors decreased by 68%. The system identified that rushed empathy statements without follow-up action were a key indicator of false hustle.
- Genuine Service Improvement: Scores for empathy effectiveness increased by 42% and problem-solving effectiveness increased by 37%.
- Customer Satisfaction: Overall CSAT scores improved by 28%.
- Agent Performance: 92% of agents showed improvement in at least one key area of genuine service delivery.
- Training Efficiency: Time to identify and address performance issues reduced from weeks to days.

Key Insights:

1. Empathy Patterns: OttoQA uncovered that the most effective empathy wasn't about using specific phrases, but about adapting tone and language to match the customer's emotional state. Agents who did this consistently had 30% higher resolution rates.
2. Problem-Solving Techniques: The system identified that agents who used analogies and real-life examples to explain complex issues had 25% higher customer understanding scores.

3. False Hustle Indicators: OttoQA discovered subtle false hustle behaviors, such as agents rushing through explanations after expressing empathy, which human QA had often missed.
4. Conversation Flow: The AI analysis revealed that interactions with a natural back-and-forth rhythm, rather than long agent monologues, were perceived as more genuine by customers.
5. Continuous Improvement: With 100% of calls analyzed, SmartMart could quickly identify emerging issues and adjust training programs in near-real-time, leading to a 40% reduction in repeat calls.

Cost Impact: SmartMart's investment in OttoQA yielded significant returns. Within the first quarter of implementation, the company observed a 65% reduction in QA-related costs, primarily due to the elimination of manual scoring for most interactions. By the end of the first year, this efficiency translated into a 78% overall cost reduction in their QA operations.

These savings were strategically reinvested into enhancing customer service technologies and expanding agent development programs, further amplifying the positive impact of the Auto QA implementation.

Conclusion: The adoption of OttoQA at SmartMart marked a transformative shift in their approach to quality assurance. Beyond merely improving accuracy and consistency, it fostered a culture deeply rooted in genuine service.

The system's ability to provide comprehensive, data-driven

insights enabled the company to swiftly identify and address false hustle behaviors, leading to marked improvements in both customer satisfaction and agent performance.

Most importantly, it allowed SmartMart to understand and enhance the nuanced aspects of customer interactions, such as empathy and problem-solving, at a scale and depth that was previously impossible. This case study illustrates that when companies leverage advanced Auto QA technology, they can create a QA framework that goes beyond performance assessment, actively discouraging false hustle and promoting authentic, effective customer interactions.

Conclusion: A New Era of QA Focused on Genuine Service

As we integrate Auto QA into our QA processes, we enter a new era where technology enables us to evaluate genuine, effective customer service at an unprecedented scale and depth. The ability to analyze every interaction deeply and consistently allows us to move beyond superficial metrics and focus on the root elements of genuine service, empowering our teams to deliver the authentic, empathetic interactions that customers truly value.

This technology doesn't just help us identify false hustle – it provides the insights needed to foster a culture of genuine service across the entire organization. By embracing Auto QA, we can create call centers that are not only more efficient but also more deeply attuned to the nuances of human interaction and the true needs of our customers.

As we look to the future, the challenge will be to continuously refine our understanding of genuine service and ensure our Auto QA systems evolve to capture ever more nuanced aspects of customer interactions. By doing so, we can stay at the forefront of delivering exceptional, authentic customer experiences in an increasingly complex service landscape.

14

The "false hustle" Antidote: Your Step-by-Step Guide to Genuine Service

When companies come to Expivia for consulting, outsourcing, or to our OttoQa company looking for assistance with their quality assurance programs, we often find ourselves tasked with completely reworking their CX approach.

The action plan I'm about to share with you is not just theoretical, it's the battle tested roadmap we use to transform customer experience programs from the ground up. Whether we're overhauling an in-house operation, integrating a client's processes into our outsourced solutions, or revamping a QA system, this comprehensive plan has proven invaluable in driving real, lasting change.

It's designed to be adaptable, allowing for the unique needs and challenges of each organization while maintaining a core focus on eliminating false hustle and fostering genuine customer service.

This plan is the culmination of years of experience, trial and error, and continuous refinement. It's structured to guide you through each phase of the transformation process, from initial assessment to long-term sustainability.

As we dive into the details, remember that this isn't just about implementing new metrics or technologies, it's about fundamentally shifting the culture and mindset of your entire customer service operation. Let's begin the journey of transforming your CX program into one that truly puts the customer first and banishes false hustle for good.

I. Introduction

- **Recap the detrimental effects of false hustle.**
- **Emphasize the need for a cultural shift to the team**: Explain why simply changing processes isn't enough to combat false hustle. A deeper cultural shift is required where the organization values genuine, customer centric service over mere speed or superficial metrics. Stress the importance of leadership buy-in and consistent messaging to foster this cultural transformation.
- **Preview the phased approach**: Introduce the phased approach that will guide the organization from recognizing and eliminating false hustle to fully embracing and sustaining a genuine service culture. Outline the benefits, including improved customer satisfaction, higher employee engagement, and long-term business success.

II. Phase 1: Identifying False Hustle in Your Organization (1-2 months)

A. **Conduct a comprehensive false hustle audit**

- **Analyze existing KPIs**: Review key performance indicators that might inadvertently encourage false hustle, such as Average Handle Time (AHT) or too much emphases on efficiency metrics. Identify which metrics drive behavior that prioritizes speed over quality.
- **Review customer complaints**: Examine customer feedback and complaints for signs of rushed or superficial service. Look for patterns that indicate service representatives are prioritizing speed over meeting the customer's actual needs.
- **Evaluate current QA processes**: Assess your quality assurance scorecards to see if there's an over-emphasis on efficiency metrics, potentially at the cost of service quality and customer satisfaction.
- **Assess employee burnout**: Conduct surveys or interviews to gauge employee burnout levels and explore how they may be linked to the pressure of maintaining high-efficiency metrics, which contribute to false hustle practices.

B. **Build a "Genuine Service Transformation" team**

- **Include naturally customer-centric members**: Select team members who have demonstrated a strong commitment to authentic customer service. These individuals can serve as role models and champions of the new approach.
- **Appoint a senior executive champion**: Ensure that a senior leader is visibly supporting the initiative, helping to drive the transformation from the top down. This executive should advocate for the shift from false hustle to genuine

service and provide the necessary resources and support.

C. **Set clear goals for eliminating false hustle**

- **Define specific false hustle behaviors**: Identify and clearly define the behaviors that exemplify false hustle within your organization, such as prioritizing quantity over quality, cutting corners to meet quotas, or focusing on metrics that don't align with customer satisfaction.
- **Establish genuine service metrics**: Develop new metrics that reflect the organization's commitment to genuine service. These could include customer satisfaction scores, problem resolution rates, or metrics that assess the quality of customer interactions rather than just their speed.

III. **Phase 2: Pilot Program – Cultivating Genuine Service**
A. **Select a pilot area most impacted by false hustle**

- Choose a team or department/team/or skill(queue) where false hustle behaviors are most prevalent, and where the impact of changing these behaviors can be most readily observed and measured.

B. **Implement new genuine service metrics and processes**

- **Revise the QA scorecard**: Shift the focus of quality assurance scorecards from efficiency metrics to measures that prioritize authenticity, customer satisfaction, and problem-solving. Ensure that agents are evaluated on their ability to connect with customers and provide solutions that address their needs.

- **De-emphasize false hustle metrics**: Significantly reduce the emphasis of metrics like AHT that incentivize speed over service quality. Encourage agents to take the time necessary to fully understand and resolve customer issues.

C. Provide intensive training on genuine service techniques

- **Focus on active listening and empathy**: Train staff on the importance of listening to customers and responding with true empathy, rather than rushing to close calls or complete tasks. This training should emphasize the value of understanding customer needs and providing tailored solutions and should go over the techniques we talked about in earlier chapters.
- **Train supervisors on coaching for genuine service**: Equip supervisors with the skills to coach their teams on providing genuine service. This includes helping them recognize and reward behaviors that align with the new service standards, and guiding them away from old habits that prioritize efficiency over customer experience.

D. Gather data on the impact of removing false hustle pressures

- Collect quantitative and qualitative data to measure the effects of the pilot. This could include changes in customer satisfaction scores, employee engagement levels, and overall service quality. Use this data to identify what's working and what may need adjustment before rolling out the changes organization-wide.

IV. Phase 3: Contact Center-wide False Hustle Elimination
A. Develop a rollout plan for genuine service adoption

- Create a detailed plan for expanding the pilot program's success across the entire contact center. This should include timelines, resource allocation, and milestones for tracking progress.

B. Systematically remove false hustle incentives across all departments

- Review and revise incentive structures, KPIs, and performance metrics in every department to ensure they no longer promote false hustle. Replace them with metrics that support genuine service and customer satisfaction.

C. Implement comprehensive genuine service training programs

- Roll out the training programs developed in the pilot phase across the organization. Ensure that every employee, from front-line staff to senior management, understands and embraces the principles of genuine service.

D. Address resistance to moving away from efficiency-focused metrics

- Anticipate and manage resistance to these changes, especially from those who may be concerned about the impact on productivity or performance. Communicate the long-term benefits of genuine service and provide support to

help teams adjust. BE PREPARED OF THIS!
- Develop a Proactive Communication Strategy
- Create a clear, compelling narrative about the need for change
- Highlight specific examples of how false hustle harms both customers and employees
- Prepare tailored messages for different stakeholder groups (e.g., agents, supervisors, executives)

V. Phase 4: Reinforcing Genuine Service Culture (Ongoing)

A. **Continuously monitor for resurgence of false hustle behaviors**

- Establish ongoing monitoring systems to detect any re-emergence of false hustle behaviors. Regularly review performance data and employee feedback to ensure the organization stays on track.

B. **Refine genuine service metrics based on customer feedback**

- Use customer feedback to continually refine and improve the metrics and processes associated with genuine service. Ensure that these metrics remain aligned with customer expectations and organizational goals.

C. **Implement rewards system for authentic customer interactions**

- Develop and implement a rewards system that recognizes and celebrates employees who exemplify genuine service.

This could include financial incentives, public recognition, or career advancement opportunities.

D. Foster a culture of continuous genuine service improvement

- Encourage a mindset of continuous improvement within the organization. Promote regular discussions about how to enhance service quality, and empower employees to suggest and implement their own ideas for better serving customers.

VI. Overcoming Obstacles in Eliminating False Hustle
A. Addressing deeply ingrained efficiency-first mindsets

- Work to shift the deeply ingrained belief that efficiency is the most important metric. Use data, success stories, and clear communication to demonstrate the value of genuine service over efficiency-first approaches.

B. Managing concerns about decreased productivity

- Reassure stakeholders that while productivity metrics may initially shift, the focus on genuine service will lead to better long-term outcomes, including higher customer loyalty and reduced employee turnover.

C. Balancing genuine service with business needs

- Find the right balance between maintaining business performance and prioritizing genuine service. This may involve adjusting targets or redefining what success looks like for different roles within the organization.

D. Maintaining commitment to genuine service under pressure

- Ensure that the commitment to genuine service remains strong, even during busy periods or when the organization is under pressure to deliver results. Reinforce the message that genuine service leads to sustainable success.

VII. Long-term Strategies for a False Hustle Free Organization
A. Embedding genuine service into company DNA

- Integrate genuine service principles into the core values, mission, and vision of the contact center.

B. Developing leaders who champion authentic customer interactions

- Invest in leadership development programs that emphasize the importance of genuine service. Cultivate leaders who model authentic customer interactions and inspire their teams to do the same.

C. Staying adaptable to maintain genuine service as customer expectations evolve

- Regularly assess and adapt to changing customer expectations. Stay ahead of industry trends and ensure that the organization's approach to genuine service evolves to meet new challenges and opportunities.

D. **Leveraging technology to support, not replace, genuine human interactions**

- Use technology to enhance, not replace, human interactions. Invest in tools that help employees deliver better service without compromising the personal touch that customers value.

VIII. Conclusion

- **Recap the journey from false hustle to genuine service**:

Summarize the key steps and phases of the transformation journey, emphasizing the shift from a focus on efficiency to a commitment to genuine service.

- **Emphasize the ongoing vigilance needed to prevent false hustle resurgence**:

Reinforce the idea that eliminating false hustle is not a one-time effort but requires continuous attention and adaptation to maintain the gains achieved.

- **Encourage readers to commit to authentic, customer-centric service**:

Call to action for leaders and organizations to fully commit to this transformation, highlighting the long term benefits of creating a culture that values and rewards genuine, customer centric service.

As we've outlined in this chapter, setting up your 'False Hustle' antidote is not just about implementing new processes or technologies. It's about fundamentally rethinking how you approach customer service—from the way you evaluate your agents to the way you measure success. This shift requires a combination of practical tools, like revamped QA scorecards and customer-centric training, and a cultural transformation that prioritizes genuine service over superficial metrics.

The antidote to false hustle is rooted in a deep commitment to solving real problems, building authentic connections, and delivering meaningful outcomes. It's not a quick fix—it's a strategic, long-term shift in how you operate. But once you put this antidote in place, the results will speak for themselves: loyal customers, more engaged employees, and a contact center that drives real value for your business.

15

Sealing the Deal: Turning Lessons into Action for Long-Term CX Success

As we reach the conclusion of our journey through the landscape of customer service, we stand at the precipice of a new era - one where false hustle is relegated to the annals of history, and genuine, impactful customer experiences take center stage. Throughout this book, we've peeled back the layers of an industry in transition, exposing the hollow practices that have long masqueraded as efficiency and unveiling the transformative power of authentic human connection.

The Fall of False Hustle

We began by shining a light on the insidious nature of false hustle - those superficial actions and metrics that create an illusion of productivity while failing to deliver real value to customers. We've seen how this mindset permeates every level of contact center operations, from frontline agents rushing through calls to executives clinging to outdated KPIs that prioritize speed over substance.

But more importantly, we've charted a course away from these detrimental practices. We've explored strategies for identifying false hustle in our own organizations, techniques for calming irate customers with genuine empathy, and methods for fostering a culture of authentic service that resonates throughout every customer interaction.

The Rise of Genuine Service

As we've dismantled the false hustle paradigm, we've simultaneously built a new framework for customer experience - one rooted in emotional intelligence, active listening, and a deep commitment to solving customer problems. We've reimagined quality assurance, transforming it from a checkbox exercise into a powerful tool for cultivating meaningful customer relationships.

The journey hasn't been easy. We've grappled with the challenges of changing ingrained behaviors, of balancing efficiency with quality, and of leveraging technology to enhance rather than replace human connection. But through it all, a new vision of customer service has emerged - one that promises not just satisfied customers, but loyal advocates who feel truly seen, heard, and valued.

The Promise of AI-Powered Quality Assurance

As we look to the future, we find ourselves on the cusp of a revolution in quality assurance. The advent of AI-powered Auto QA tools represents not just an incremental improvement in our ability to monitor and improve customer interactions, but a quantum leap in our capacity to understand and enhance the customer experience.

Imagine a world where every single customer interaction is analyzed not just for adherence to scripts or handling times, but for the depth of empathy displayed, the effectiveness of problem-solving, and the genuine human connection fostered. With Auto QA, this world is not just possible - it's imminent.

These tools offer us unprecedented insights into the nuances of customer interactions, allowing us to:

1. Identify patterns of successful engagement that human analysts might miss
2. Provide real-time coaching and support to agents, enabling them to deliver better service in the moment
3. Continuously refine our understanding of what constitutes truly exceptional customer service
4. Scale our quality assurance efforts to cover 100% of interactions without sacrificing depth of analysis

But make no mistake - the rise of AI in quality assurance is not about replacing human judgment. Rather, it's about augmenting our human capabilities, freeing up our teams to focus on the higher-level analysis and strategic thinking that drive real innovation in customer experience.

The Road Ahead

As we stand at this crossroads, the path forward is clear. The future of customer experience lies not in faster handle times or more rigid scripts, but in the cultivation of genuine human connections, powered by emotional intelligence and supported by cutting-edge technology.

To thrive in this new landscape, organizations must:

1. Embrace a culture of continuous learning and improvement, always seeking to deepen our understanding of customer needs and expectations
2. Invest in the emotional intelligence of our teams, recognizing that empathy and authentic communication are skills that can be developed and refined
3. Leverage AI and automation not as replacements for human interaction, but as tools to enhance and elevate the quality of our customer engagements
4. Reimagine our metrics and KPIs to align with what truly matters to customers - not just speed and efficiency, but genuine problem resolution and positive emotional outcomes
5. Foster a sense of ownership and pride in customer service at every level of the organization, from the C-suite to the frontline

The dawn of authentic customer experience is upon us. As we bid farewell to false hustle and embrace a future of genuine, impactful service, we open the door to unprecedented levels of customer loyalty, employee satisfaction, and business success.

The question is no longer whether we can afford to make this transition, but whether we can afford not to. The organizations that thrive in the coming years will be those that recognize the immense value of authentic human connection and harness the power of technology to deliver it consistently and at scale.

As you close this book, I challenge you to become a champion of this new era in your own organization. Embrace the principles we've explored, challenge the status quo, and lead the charge towards a future where every customer interaction is an opportunity to create a genuine, lasting connection.

The future of customer experience is in your hands. Let's build it together.

16

Added Content

I hope you found value in false hustle or at least planted a seed to have to see how CX can be done differently and we this need to happen in the age of AI.

I want to make sure you get a change to check out all my other content.

LinkedIn:

If you do nothing else, please follow me on LinkedIn. I never sell, I just post contact center content that will add value, please make sure to follow!

OttoQa.com:

First off, check out ottoqa.com. See how we are reinventing how to score QA calls, the blog has a ton of AI and QA info as well.

Advice from a Call Center Geek:

I believe we have the worlds number 1 contact center podcast named "Advice from a Call Center Geek". You can find it here:

Itunes:

https://podcasts.apple.com/us/podcast/advice-from-a-call-center-geek/id1447535209

Spotify:

https://open.spotify.com/show/7ssSLPmPOsuk63DsED2Pa1

Expivia:

If you are looking for USA contact center outsourcing, please check out our BPO Expivia at expiviausa.com

TikTok:

We post daily/weekly contact center content on TikTok, follow us at https://www.tiktok.com/@callcenter_geek?is_from_we bapp=1&sender_device=pc

www.ingramcontent.com/pod-product-compliance
Lightning Source LLC
Chambersburg PA
CBHW070928210326
41520CB00021B/6838